The Chiltern Hills

Exploring the Notable and Unusual

21 Circular Walks

Each with a fine pub on the way

Martyn Loach

AMERWEB PUBLISHING, AMERSHAM,
BUCKINGHAMSHIRE

First Published 2012
Second Edition 2014

© Martyn Loach 2012

For Mom

All rights reserved

INTRODUCTION

Welcome to the second edition of the definitive walking guide to the notable and unusual features of the Chiltern Hills, an area of outstanding natural beauty. Glorious viewpoints and historic houses might be the best known attractions but what about the more unusual? A totem pole in Berkhamsted, the water well donated by an Indian maharajah in Stoke Row or a memorial to a crashed bomber near Stokenchurch, all will add interest, curiosity and poignancy to a walk.

These 21 circular walks, the majority of which have shorter versions, are structured around such features and all include an excellent pub, some with a story to tell of their own. Pubs though are closing at such an alarming rate that two featured in the first edition of this book have already ceased to trade (alternatives have been found and one new walk devised). Others have closed only to thankfully re-open, so I recommend you visit them sooner rather than later.

Generally, the walks follow Public Footpaths and Bridleways. Roads are kept to an absolute minimum and any lanes will be quiet (in inclement weather they might be a welcome alternative to a muddy bridleway). Long walking routes are shown as a solid red line with any adjoining Public Footpaths and Bridleways marked as short red dashes. Alternative short routes are indicated by long magenta dashes. Note that maps in this book include certain tarmac surfaced roads and lanes for reference but not tracks.

All large gates are described as 5bar, whether they have 4, 6 or any number of bars. It is also worth bearing in mind that the countryside is always changing and some waymarks and features such as telephone boxes or signposts may well have changed or moved location. In particular, stiles are increasingly replaced by gates. In fact very few stiles remain on these walks and much of this change has come about through the excellent work of the Chiltern Society.

It is recommended that you take an appropriate Ordnance Survey map. The walks are all contained within the 171 Chiltern Hills West, 172 Chiltern Hills East and 181 Chiltern Hills North Explorer editions. Although directions are clear and you shouldn't get lost, any doubts will be resolved if you can refer to an OS map.

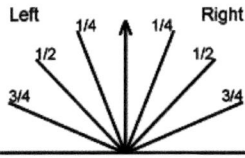

For ease, instead of compass points or other directional methods that need more than a passing knowledge of navigation, paths may be referred to as ¼ (22.5°), ½ (45°) or ¾ (67.5°) left or right of the direction in which you are walking.

3

CONTENTS

Amersham 8¼ or 1¾ miles	Ruth Ellis' Grave, Martyrs' Memorial, High & Over, Stiff Leadbetter House	6
Ashridge 6¾ or 4½ miles	Bridgewater Monument, Grand Union Canal, Aldbury Nowers Nature Reserve	12
Berkhamsted 7¼ or 4 miles	Totem Pole, Berkhamsted Castle, 'Roman Road', Frithsden Vineyard	17
Bix Bottom 5¼ or 3¾ miles	Warburg Nature Reserve, Nettlebed Brick Kiln, Berrick Trench SSI	23
Chinnor 7 or 4 miles	Narrow Gauge Railway, Nature Reserves, Archaeological Sites, Midsomer Murders' Pub	28
Cholesbury 5½ or 4¼ miles	Iron Age Fort, 12th Century Manor, Highest Chilterns' Pub	33
Coombe Hill 7¾ or 5½ miles	Chilterns' Highest Viewpoint, Chequers, Iron Age Fort, Whiteleaf Cross, Nature Reserve	38
Ewelme 7¾ or 3¾ miles	Water Cress Beds, Author's Grave, Two Historic Churches	44
Gt Missenden 6¼ or 3¾ miles	Roald Dahl Museum and Story Centre, Liberty Figurehead, Balloon Club	49
Hambleden 7½ or 6 miles	Winery and Brewery, Deer Park	54
Ivinghoe 5½ miles	Britain's Oldest Post Mill, Ivinghoe Beacon, Ford End Water Mill	60
Jordans 9¼ or 7¼ miles	Quaker Estate, Captain Cook Memorial, Milton's Cottage	65
Lacey Green 7½ or 3½ miles	Rupert Brooke's Local, Lacey Green Windmill, John Hampden Monument and Grave	70
Latimer & Chenies 6 miles	A Horse's Grave, Chenies Manor	76
Marsworth 8 or 5½ miles	Grand Union Canal, Reservoirs, Wendover Arm Restoration, Nature Reserve	82

Rotherfield Greys 7 or 4¼ miles	Greys Court	86
Stoke Row 7¾ or 3½ miles	Maharajah's Well, Philanthropist's House	91
Stokenchurch 9 or 7¼ miles	Bluebell Woods, Bomber Memorial, Red Kites, Getty's Cricket Ground, Nature Reserve	97
Turville 5 or 3 miles	TV & Film Locations inc. Vicar of Dibley Church, Chitty Chitty Bang Bang Windmill	102
West Wycombe 4 miles	Hell-Fire Caves, Church and Mausoleum, Disraeli Manor, National Trust Villages	107
Whipsnade 4¾ or 3 miles	Tree Cathedral, War Memorial, Bronze Age Burial Site, Nature Reserve	113

FEATURED PUBS

Amersham: *The Red Lion, The Crown Inn (both Little Missenden),
The Eagle (Old Amersham)*
Ashridge: *The Valiant Trooper, The Greyhound (both Aldbury)*
Berkhamsted: *The Alford Arms (Frithsden)*
Bix Bottom: *The White Hart (Nettlebed),
The Five Horseshoes (Maidensgrove)*
Chinnor: *The Lions of Bledlow (Bledlow)*
Cholesbury: *The White Lion (St Leonards)*
Coombe Hill: *The Russell Arms (Butlers Cross)*
Ewelme: *Shepherds Hut, The Red Lion (Britwell Salome)*
Great Missenden: *The Black Horse*
Hambleden: *The Frog (Skirmett)*
Ivinghoe: *The Village Swan (Ivinghoe Aston)*
Jordans: *Merlin's Cave (Chalfont St Giles)*
Lacey Green: *The Whip Inn, Pink & Lily (Parslow's Hillock)*
Latimer: *The Cock (Sarratt)*
Marsworth: *The Red Lion, Grand Junction Arms (Bulbourne)*
Rotherfield Greys: *The Maltsters Arms,
The Red Lion (Peppard Common)*
Stokenchurch: *Fox & Hounds (Christmas Common)*
Stoke Row: *The Black Horse (Scot's Common), The Crown (Nuffield)*
Turville: *The Bull and Butcher*
West Wycombe: *The Red Lion (Bradenham)*
Whipsnade: *Old Hunters Lodge*

Amersham

Ruth Ellis' Grave, Martyrs' Memorial, High & Over, Stiff Leadbetter House

Martyrs' Memorial

The best starting place for this walk is St Mary's Church. Take the path that leads past the vicarage at the east end and cross the small bridge over the Misbourne. Turn right onto the Chiltern Heritage Trail. On the left is the graveyard (1) that is the final resting place of Ruth Ellis, the last woman to be hanged in England.

There is no headstone, although a little research will pinpoint the grave's location.

At the far end of the graveyard (past a wooden bridge and uphill along a narrow path) there is a signpost to the Martyr's (sic) Memorial ¾ left.

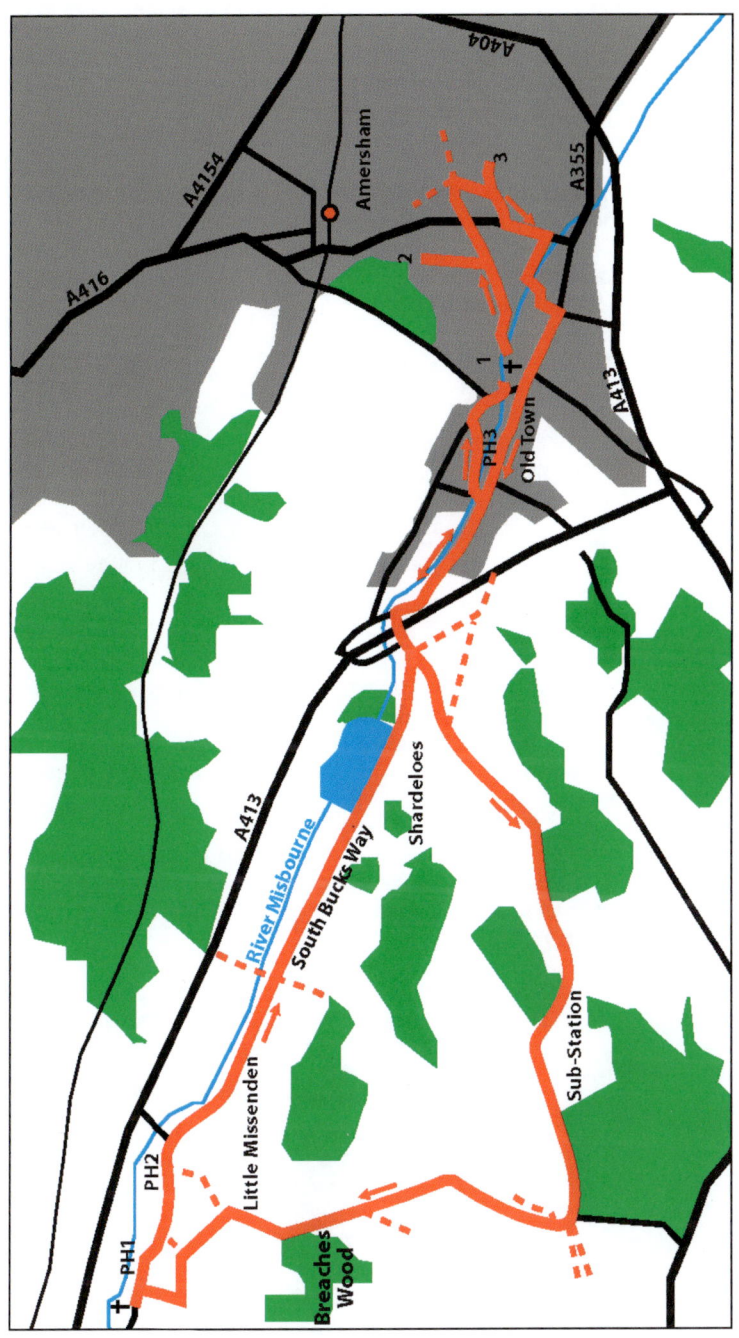

When you reach the brow of the hill you can see the memorial on your left (2). Continue to a signpost on the edge of the field and then go left to reach it. The memorial commemorates several Protestant martyrs put to death at a nearby spot in 1521 for their beliefs that included, much to the church's consternation, reading the bible in English.

Retrace your steps to the footpath signpost and turn left through the hedge and descend to Station Road. Cross straight over and climb to where this path meets three others. Turn right and, after you cross a quiet residential road, there is a house on the left that gives you an indication of the architectural importance of the area.

At the next road - Highover Park - turn left uphill and amongst a rather undistinguished housing estate you will find no. 42, named High & Over (3).

Perhaps in a moment of hyperbole, John Betjemin described this reinforced concrete structure in a Y shape by Amyas Connell, as 'scandalizing the whole of Buckinghamshire' when it was built. It is one of the first 'modernist' houses in the country, later to be joined by others in the locality, and has been described rather pompously as a 'complex reworking of Corbusean modernism'. Saved from demolition in 1962, the house is now a Grade II* listed building.

Turn back and continue to the bottom of the road and there are more 'Sun Houses' to admire. Turn left onto the main road opposite Ruckles Way and then, just past a pedestrian crossing, go right signposted the Chiltern Heritage Trail.

At the end of the tarmac track, turn left over a footbridge and go to the

front of Tesco. Use the pedestrian crossing, go to the right of Fox's and cross over to the petrol station side of the road. Diagonally left over the traffic island is Bury Farm where William Penn (see Jordans walk) courted Gulielma Springett before heading off to America,

Now walk towards Old Amersham and then along a High Street that is an attractive mixture of different architectural styles.

8

There is much to admire including a 1783 Baptist Chapel behind the Kings Arms and the 1657 almshouses, in addition to plenty of pubs and restaurants for refreshment.

If you only fancy a short walk, call it a day in Amersham Old Town. Otherwise, continue all the way through the town, onward past the last house until the path on the left side leaves the road and reaches the very busy bypass (you can hear it before seeing it). Cross to a lane on the other side hidden behind bushes and bear right to the entrance to the Shardeloes Estate.

Go to the left of the beautifully located cricket pitch and follow the drive uphill until just before the concealed entrance of Lower Park House. Here turn left along a hedge and pass a row of show jumping fences.

The path becomes a track and then back to grass. Keep straight, there is no need to go off right or left. Just before the end of the final field you leave the hedge on the left, bearing slightly right to go through a gap in the hedge in front of you. Go right along a narrow path through an area that's great for blackberries in September. You now climb following an old wooden fence and drainage ditch. You will go under a line of pylons leading to a large electricity sub-station hidden on your left. After a second line, you turn right along the edge of a wood that is carpeted with bluebells during the spring.

Continue straight when you reach a broken fence and turn right when you get to Mop End Lane. At the entrance to Mop End Farm go over a stile (ignoring an adjacent bridleway) and the path goes ¼ left towards the far end of a line of ash trees.

At the stile go right and follow the hedge under a row of pylons. When you get to a field boundary hedge that doesn't quite reach the track you're on, there's a wooden footpath post directing you diagonally across the next field. Go through a field boundary and keep straight on to the next stile (or follow the hedge to the left if you don't want to trample the crops).

Turn right onto Toby's Lane that, at this point, is a narrow bridleway. After skirting Breaches Wood, you will start glimpsing Little Missenden through the hedge on the left. Look out for a metal gate and then take the clear well used path downhill across the field to Beamond End Lane. Now turn right past Town Farm Cottage.

At the road junction go left to admire the wall paintings of Little Missenden church or right to the 16th century Red Lion (PH1) that survived a severe fire in 2006 and now offers good food and live music.

Continue through this attractive, well-heeled village until just after The Crown Inn (PH2) and then go right along the South Bucks Way. This is a clear wide track that turns to grass and runs parallel to the A413 and the River Misbourne all the way to Shardeloes (about 1 mile / 1.6 kms).

Shardeloes dates from 1758. Built by the marvellously named Stiff Leadbetter, it was formally the seat of the Drake family and has seen time as a maternity hospital whose most famous product was probably Sir Tim Rice.

Passing Shardeloes you reach the cricket pitch again. Go to the left of the pavilion and through the entrance gate. Retrace your route across the bypass and towards Old Amersham.

Instead of going all through the town look out for Mill Lane on your left, go over the Misbourne and immediately turn right following the river behind the High Street. If you so desire, a footbridge conveniently crosses the river to The Eagle (PH3).

10

If not, continue until you reach a wooden fence and the brick wall of a collection of old brewery buildings. Follow the wall around to the entrance of what is now The Maltings Craft Workshops and unfortunately no longer the maltings of Wellers Brewery.

Bear left up to School Lane and then right to a mini roundabout, go right again and you will return to the church.

Starting Point: St. Mary's Church

SU958973
Explorer Map 172
Chiltern Hills East

Length:

Urban and Rural Walk: 8¼ miles / 13.2 kilometres
Urban Walk around Amersham: 1¾ miles / 2.9 kilometres

Terrain:

The Amersham part of the walk includes uphill sections, while the 'rural' section is largely undemanding after climbing past Shardeloes.

Ashridge

Bridgewater Monument, Grand Union Canal, Aldbury Nowers Nature Reserve

Bridgewater Monument

The Ashridge Estate, that covers 5000 acres / 2025 ha, is a varied landscape that includes woodlands and chalk downlands containing a rich mixture of flora and fauna.

The Bridgewater Monument commemorates Francis, third Duke of Bridgewater - the Father of Inland Navigation – who ironically had nothing to do with the nearby Grand Union. It is 108 ft / 33 mtrs tall and was erected in 1832. Climb the 170 steps on a summer weekend and you will have a marvellous view of the surrounding countryside.

From its entrance go behind the monument and take the path that proclaims 'No Mobility Vehicles Beyond This Point'. After the sign, descend, bear right and, after passing Tim's Spring, you must bear left downhill.

12

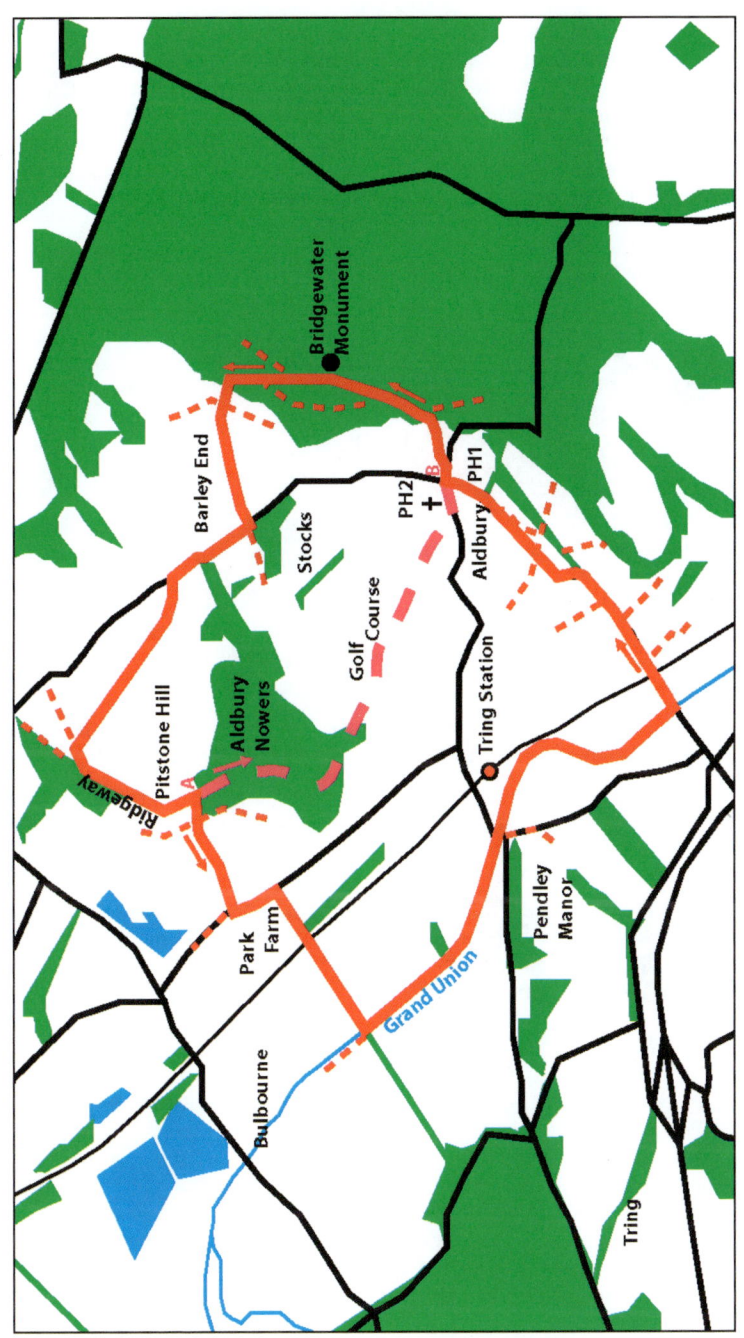

When you reach an open field, follow the hedge on your left. This bridleway winds down through stables and you will reach the lane from Ivinghoe to Aldbury. Turn right onto the lane. Continue past Golding's Spring opposite a dead end. Walk for another 250 yds / mtrs and look out for a footpath on the left through a gap in the hedge. The path bears right following the hedge on your left. Leave the field edge when it bends left and keep virtually straight on across the field.

This is quite a well used path and is usually easy to follow especially in the summer when crops are growing. There is an insignificant post at the next field boundary that will help to guide you. Continue in the same direction across the following field and go right when you reach the field edge to a stile.

At the stile turn left onto The Ridgeway that follows the edge of Pitstone Hill.

Pass a line of weatherbeaten hawthorns with Ivinghoe, its ugly sister Pitstone and its quarry, on your right. When you reach a track going left, follow the bridleway straight on. This is Grim's Ditch, an earthwork that possibly dates from the Iron Age and runs for 19 mls / 30 kms through the Chilterns. The track goes downhill, then left and reaches a kissing gate. This is Point A.

Short Walk from Point A

Keep straight on through the kissing gate along the clearly marked Ridgeway. This is an attractive woodland walk through the nature reserve with fine views. After just over ½ mile / 0.8 km you will descend some steps, with a footpath going off to the right, to reach a junction of paths. Here you leave The Ridgeway by going left and then after a short distance right. When you reach open ground there is a finger post and crossing bridleway. Keep straight on the footpath that crosses Stocks golf course on a marked path. At the far side continue straight along a path to Aldbury.

Turn left when you get to the lane into Aldbury passing the parish church. By the 13th century, St John the Baptist, was virtually how you see it today. Inside, the Pendley Chapel is enclosed by the only stone screen in the Chilterns. Continue to the village green which is Point B.

For the long walk, turn right before the kissing gate, leaving The Ridgeway. Ignore the stile immediately on the left, continue downhill (adjacent to Aldbury Nowers Nature Reserve) and you will go through a metal gate (where another footpath goes right). Passing a bridleway off to the left, you will reach and go through three metal barriers before getting to a fairly busy road. Turn left onto the road and go for 350 yds / 320 mtrs until you see a sign for 'Public Restricted Byway 62' and the Grand Union Canal.

Cross the road, walk down the concrete drive and through stables. You will reach and cross the London to Birmingham railway, go past Marsh Croft Farm and eventually, by walking along the long straight tarmac driveway, you get to the London to Birmingham canal i.e. the Grand Union where you turn left onto the towpath.

The canal at this point is quiet and shaded where the ducks are occasionally scattered by leisure boats. Although watch out for bikes especially at weekends.

You now follow the towpath for about 1¾ mls / 2.8 kms.

Go under a bridge near to Tring Station and then climb up to Newground Road when you reach bridge 136. Turn right along the road towards the railway. After the railway bridge, ignore Byway 62 on the left, take the next footpath that goes left through a metal gate near to an Aldbury sign.

Go diagonally across the field to another metal gate and turn right. Follow the hedge and cross a bridleway to a kissing gate and onward to another. When you enter a small housing estate continue forward to The Valiant Trooper (PH1).

15

The pub, made up of two 17th century cottages, is so named as the Duke of Wellington may have addressed his troops there.

Carry on up Trooper Road to the green and The Greyhound (PH2), more upmarket and attractively covered in ivy. This is Point B.

Long and Short Walk from Point B

From the village green, complete with stocks and pond, follow the sign for Gaddesden and Berkhamsted along Toms Hill Road. Just past the Aldbury Peace Memorial Institute turn left onto a bridleway marked 'Bridgewater Monument ½' following the Hertfordshire Way.

Climb fairly steeply, ignoring any bridleways off to the left and right, until reaching and turning left onto the Ashridge Estate Boundary Trail to return to the monument.

Starting Point: Bridgewater Monument

SP968131
Explorer Map 181
Chiltern Hills North

Length:

Long Walk: 6¾ miles / 10.9 kilometres
Short Walk: 4½ miles / 7.25 kilometres

Terrain:

A varied walk with lots of fine views and lovely woodland. No serious hills until a steep climb back to the monument.

Berkhamsted

Totem Pole, Berkhamsted Castle, 'Roman Road', Frithsden Vineyard

Totem Pole, Grand Union Canal

The reason why the birthplace of the novelist Graham Greene is more than just a pleasant dot on the map is that two of the nation's major industrial arteries pass through the town on their way to Birmingham and London. The Grand Union Canal, built between 1793 and 1805, played an important part in the country's industrial growth and survived as a commercial concern until the great freeze of 1963. Today it is an attractive backwater winding through the town adjacent to George Stevenson's railway - the latter, little more than a generation later, again connected the nation's two largest cities but this time at much greater speed.

The totem pole (1) is erected next to the Grand Union, on the former J Alsford Ltd site. The company was a fencing contractor to the railway and the pole was a gift to the company from their Canadian wood suppliers in British Columbia.

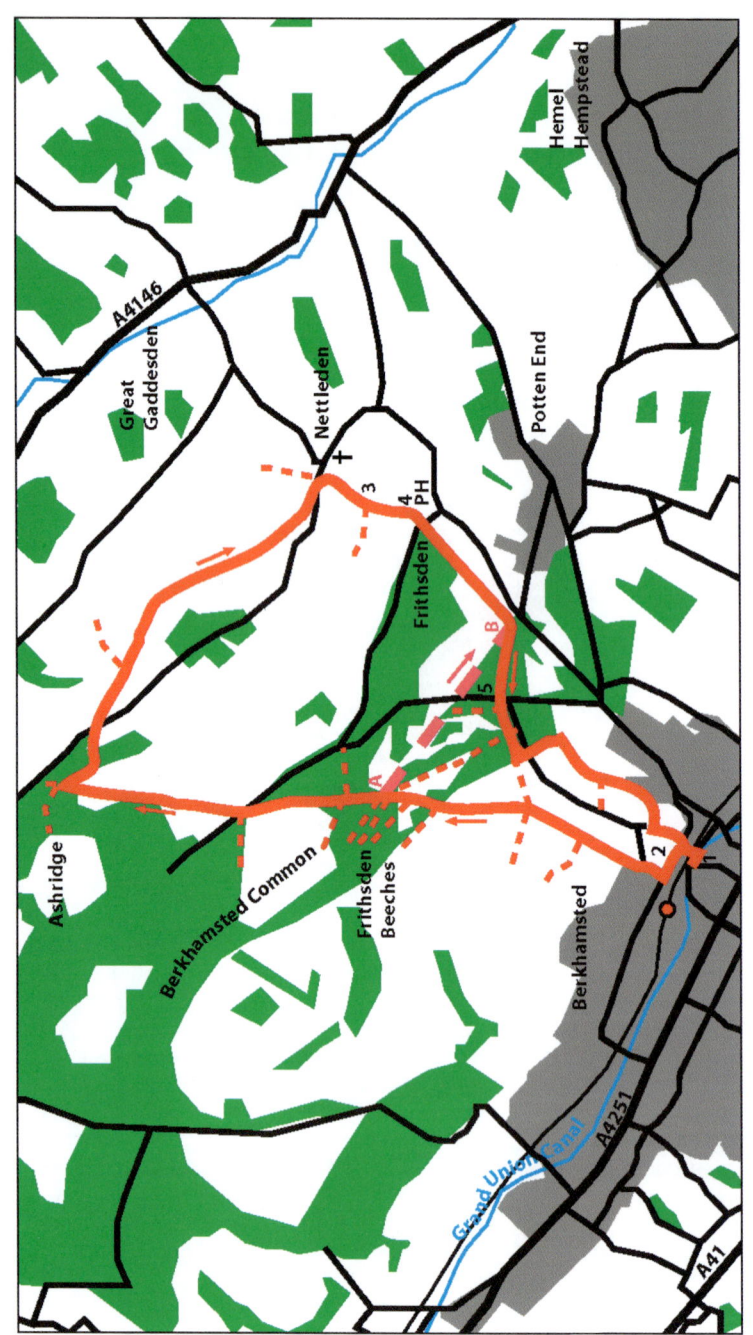

From the totem pole (opposite you have the Crystal Palace pub, designed by the same Paxton who was responsible for the one in London) go over the canal bridge and left along Lower Kings Road.

Turn right on Brownlow Road under the railway and you reach the remains of Berkhamsted Castle (2). This motte and bailey construction was built by Robert, Count of Mortain, a brother of William the Conquerer. The castle was originally surrounded by a double ditch and two moats fed by spring water but suffered from the onset of industrialization with one of the moats drained for the canal and the outer defences damaged by the arrival of the railway. Today the motte remains impressive at 50 ft / 15 mtrs high and has a fine view for anyone fit enough to climb it.

From the castle continue along Brownlow Road. When it bends right, go straight up Castle Hill and, when that road goes left, continue straight on - following a sign marked 'Berkhamsted Common 1'. This directs you through a car park, past tennis courts and onto a grass track in between sports pitches. Continue straight, ignoring one public footpath that goes left, until reaching Well Farm. Here go straight over a crossing footpath and past the farm, keeping to the left of a hedge. You will reach a field boundary with a sign for the Grand Union Circular Walk.

Follow the GUCW along the hedge up to a kissing gate into trees. Keep straight following the bridleway and GUCW signs. Climbing uphill, you follow the same signs when reaching open ground.

On entering more trees you will pass a line of three yellow topped posts. Fork right at the second post and follow the third to reach another two posts. Cross a bridleway following a GUCW sign and you'll get to a further crossing bridleway where there is a finger direction post. This is Point A.

Short Walk from Point A

Turn right onto the crossing bridleway (still marked Grand Union Circular Walk and now also Ashridge Boundary Trail and Hertfordshire Way). You will go between the 7th tee and an adjoining green on Berkhamsted golf course and enter trees where the bridleway is marked with yellow topped posts. A signpost will eventually direct you across the 4th fairway to another stake. You quickly cross the Ashridge – Berkhamsted road, continuing on the Hertfordshire Way and GUCW. Follow a fairway until, just after a footpath on the left, you take a bark path past the 16th tee. The path will go downhill through more trees towards the Nettleden Road and a path comes in from the left. This is Point B.

The long walk continues straight, along the bridleway that eventually widens through Frithsden Beeches. After crossing another bridleway (Icknield Way Trail), you get to a large expanse of open land at Berkhamsted Common and bear right on a gravel track that runs along its edge. This becomes tarmac and, when it bends downhill to a car park, you keep straight on the marked bridleway. At the next post go right to the road and cross over following the 'Little Gaddesden 1' sign.

The route is now practically straight as an arrow for ¾ mile / 1.25 kms.

The drive you initially take is also a Permissive Bridleway that will fork right, but you keep straight on and, when past Rodinghead, you follow a barbed wire fence. When this fence ends at a kissing gate keep straight, passing a tree trunk bench on your left.

This is the Golden Valley where you slowly descend along the valley side to a gate that's marked with a National Trust badge. Continue straight on and, at the bottom of the valley, you will reach a yellow topped post.

Here take the National Trust bridleway and Ashridge Estate Boundary Trail, ½ right uphill through trees and behind a fenced off area. When the track bends sharply left look out for a footpath off to the right. After clambering up the embankment you follow the path up to a recreational area, go ½ right to a garden fence then follow the path a short way before turning left through a small group of houses to the road.

Go through the gate opposite and ½ right marked 'Nettleden 1¾'. You now descend to and follow another glorious valley all the way to Nettleden. Entering Nettleden you turn first right past Pightle Cottage.

After the tarmac ends you continue uphill on the Icknield Way Trail, known locally as the 'Roman Road' (3), ignoring a footpath that forks left. Thought to be haunted by a monk, the high walls do add a certain spookiness. The bridge you go under was built by the Duke of Bridgewater as a short cut to Ashridge.

Keep straight over the top of the hill and descend to the Frithsden Vineyard (4). Originally planted in 1971, it was re-established in 2005. The wine is grown, pressed and bottled on site and sold in their shop that's open from Friday – Sunday.

A little further on is the Alford Arms (PH), a modern country pub that does excellent food. Now cross the road and follow the bridleway uphill until you reach a large house called The Grange. Cross to the footpath opposite. When the gardens end, go through a horse barrier and bear right and then turn left onto a bridleway. This is Point B.

Long and Short Walk from Point B

Go downhill to Nettleden Road and then practically double back on yourself on another bridleway. You now meander up to Berkhamsted golf course. When you reach the open go straight across a fairway into trees. Pass the 18th tee, then cautiously over two fairways following yellow topped posts to the war memorial (5). You might catch sight of the top of the memorial some way before reaching it.

The memorial commemorates the Inns of Court Training Corps who put 12,000 soldiers through their paces during the Great War. 2,000 didn't return.

From the memorial, cross over the road to the car park opposite and take the bridleway downhill. Quickly ignore a bridleway and footpath off to the right, continue downhill parallel to the road. Don't take the first bridleway on the left, turn left on the second (when the one you're on becomes a footpath) to the road. Cross and go uphill. Continue straight on the clear path even when the bridleway forks left and, at the top of the hill, turn right on Public Footpath 2 that tells you that Berkhamsted Station is 1 mile away.

Now go along the top of the field passing an old cattle grid and continue with the hedge / fence on your left and Berkhamsted clearly in view. When you reach a white building, that you will partially see in the distance, you have to go right downhill along a beech hedge, then along a further row of trees to the road. Here turn left along the footpath that follows the edge of the castle back to the town.

Starting Point: Totem Pole (nr Castle St. bridge over Grand Union)

SP994080
Explorer Map 181
Chiltern Hills North

Length:

Long Walk: 7¼ miles / 11.7 kilometres
Short Walk: 4 miles / 6.4 kilometres

Terrain:

Farmland changes to attractive woodland followed by beautiful valleys.

Bix Bottom

Warburg Nature Reserve, Nettlebed Brick Kiln, Berrick Trench SSI

Warburg Nature Reserve

The Warburg Reserve is a little hard to find but the effort is very worthwhile.

It is the flagship reserve of BBOWT (Berks, Bucks, Oxon Wildlife Trust), with all year round interest including 450 species of plant, 900 fungi species, half of the nation's butterfly species and 62 types of bird.

There is a visitor centre and a collection of short walks through differing habitats. Enter the reserve from the car park and go left following the Wildlife Walk sign. At the next sign go left again, through a gate and then right.

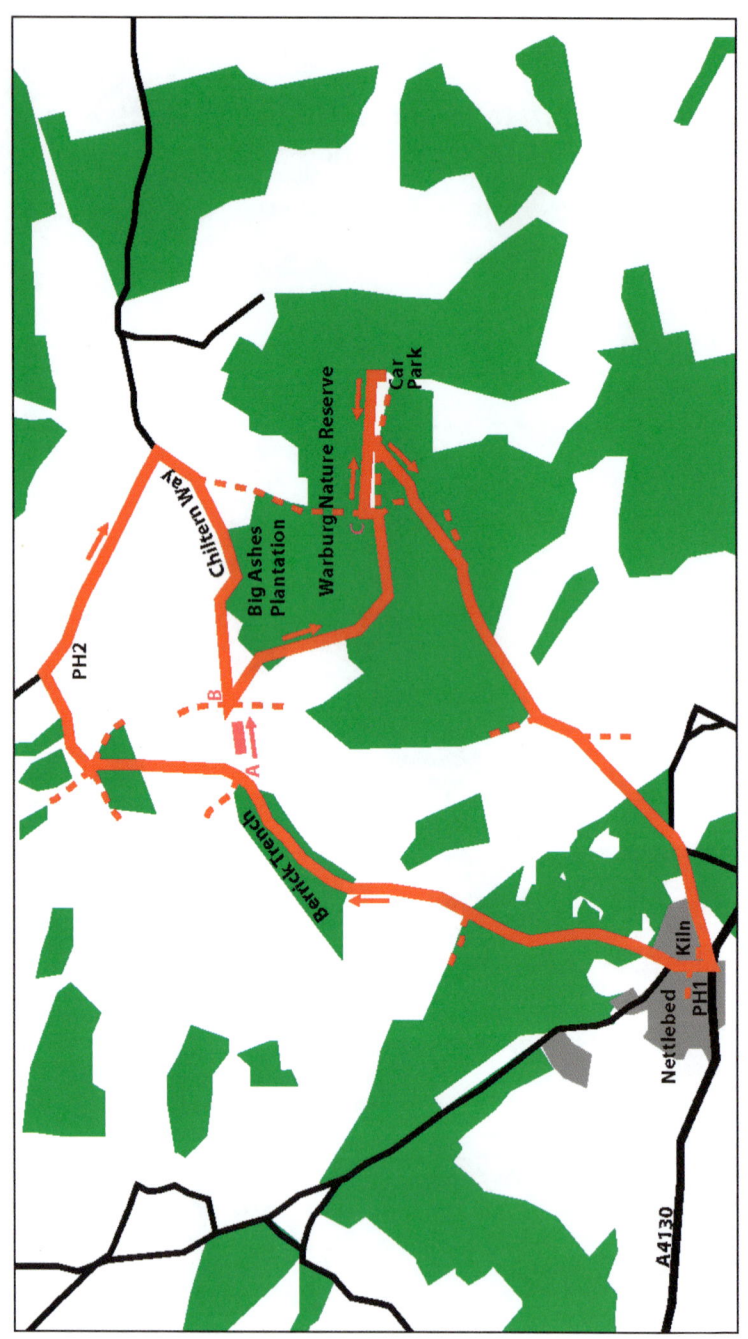

After only a few yards go left through a fence onto a public footpath. This rises through very attractive woodland and you bear left onto a restricted byway after 225 yds / 200 mtrs.

Ignoring a permissive footpath, you reach a crossroads. Go ½ right uphill on the track ahead (not right on the crossing track).

After leaving woodland, keep straight, passing a long wooden fence and then forward on the Chiltern Way Extension along a tarmac lane at Soundness House. Continue along this very quiet lane after the Chiltern Way goes off left. Then ignore a bridleway on the left and you'll reach a crossroads.

Turn right. After a short distance you'll pass Walnut Cottage and, further on, catch a glimpse of the brick kiln. Turn right when you reach The Old Kiln.

The kiln is now located rather incongruously in the middle of a neat housing estate. Flemish immigrants initiated the Chilterns' brick industry using local natural resources and this particular kiln was used from the 1700s to 1938.

Keep on towards Nettlebed and take the B481 Watlington Street. (for refreshment you can choose to carry straight on to The White Hart (PH1)).

After only a short distance the B481 bears left but you carry straight onto a bridleway that is Mill Road.

Follow this no through road and at the top of the hill the bridleway goes left into trees just before an electricity sub-station.

Look out for a tree arrow and go ¼ right when the path forks. There are further arrows to follow as you go downhill and at the bottom of the incline go ¾ right. Continue until you reach and turn right onto a track.

Just before a house and adjacent mansion, leave the bridleway and take a footpath off to the right. Pass by a pond and continue through a kissing gate. The path now hugs the field boundary before crossing the field diagonally to the far corner where you'll find another kissing gate.

You now enter trees at Berrick Trench, a Site of Special Scientific Interest. This is an ancient beech woodland that also contains ash, oak, whitebeam, field maple and hazel, a remarkable diversity of shrubs, not to mention rare plant species.

When the path reaches a kissing gate at the far side of the wood, go ¼ right as indicated along the fence to a restricted byway. This Point A.

Short Walk from Point A

For the short walk, turn right for 275 yds / 250 mtrs until you reach Point B where you go ½ right keeping on the restricted byway (SW28).

For the long walk, cross the byway to the opposite kissing gate and go ½ right across the field to another one. Now go slightly right under a line of telegraph poles. There is no clear path across the meadow, although it becomes slightly clearer as you approach trees on the other side of the field. You may also see a tree arrow on the edge of the wood. If not, bear in mind that you are heading for the far right corner of the field. To cheer you up, when you are crossing the field look very high to the right and you'll glimpse The Five Horseshoes (PH2).

At the corner of the field go left on the bridleway and quickly right onto a footpath. This is a very steep climb. At the top, follow the fence around to the right and then go left through a kissing gate, up steps then along the path to a lane. Turn right to The Five Horseshoes. This is an isolated hostelry that ticks all the right country pub boxes, with fine ales and good food.

26

From the well kept garden you have a superb view of red kites flying over the Oxfordshire countryside.

From the pub carry on along the lane until just before it bends sharply left. Here take the Chiltern Way on your right. After 175 yds / 160 mtrs, go ½ right following the Chiltern Way.

For a short cut you could go straight on until reaching Point C, but you would miss out on some pretty woodland and an outstanding viewpoint.

After crossing the field, the Chiltern Way will follow the edge of Big Ashes Plantation (part of the reserve). Once in the open again go ½ left to another kissing gate. Descend steeply down steps through more trees and you'll reach a perfect picnic bench with a fine view over the valley.

Continue ½ right downhill over the next field to a kissing gate located at Point B.

Long and Short Walk from Point B

On the long walk turn sharp left onto the restricted byway and you will soon be back in the reserve.

Turn left on SW31 that crosses the byway and then look out for the Permissive Path on your right after 50 yds / mtrs. Follow this path all the way back to the car park.

Starting Point: Warburg Nature Reserve Car Park

SU720878
Explorer Map 171
Chiltern Hills West

Length:

Long Walk: 5¼ miles / 8.45 kilometres
Short Walk: 3¾ miles / 6.04 kilometres

Terrain:

This is one of the shorter walks but is quite strenuous in places and in the winter can be muddy.

Chinnor

Narrow Gauge Railway, Nature Reserves, Archaeological Sites, Midsomer Murders' Pub

Chinnor and Princes Risborough Railway

First opened in 1872, the original Icknield Line stopped carrying passengers in 1957 and ceased operations entirely in 1989. It was then taken over by the volunteers of the Chinnor and Princes Risborough Railway who ran their first passenger service in 1994.

At present the line has a round trip of about seven miles but there are plans to extend it onward to Princess Risborough. There are services using diesel and steam trains on most Sundays, some Saturdays and Bank Holidays.

From the roundabout at the entrance to the railway (1) go up Hill Road away from Chinnor. It is only a short distance after the footpath ends to reach The Ridgeway / Icknield Way. This is Point A.

Short Walk from Point A

The short walk is really just a pleasant stroll to the pub and back. It avoids the strenuous bits but also misses the quarry and nature reserves. Turn left onto The Ridgeway / Icknield Way and follow this national trail for ¾ mile / 1.25 kms, ignoring a footpath and a crossing bridleway until you reach a second bridleway with a signpost for Chinnor Reserve and Barrows. This is Point B.

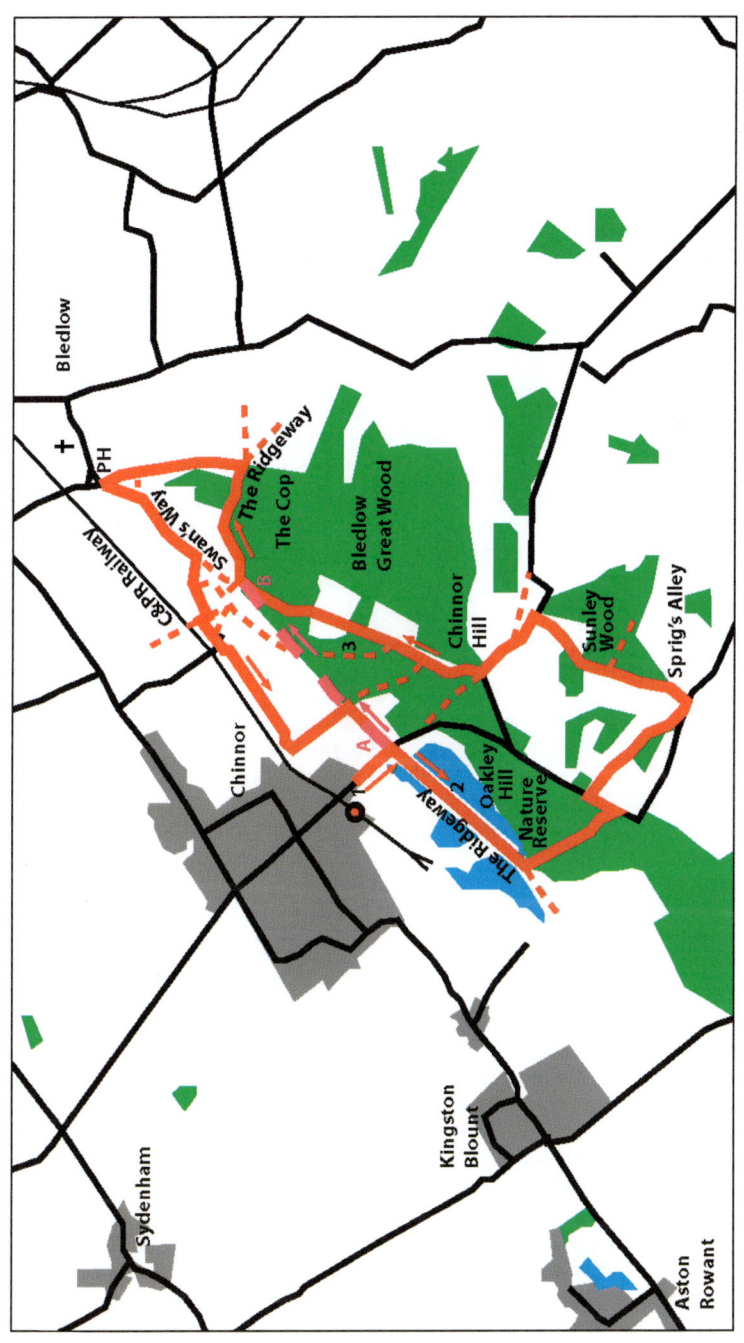

For the long walk, turn right on The Ridgeway / Icknield Way. On each side you'll glimpse the old quarries of the Chinnor cement works (2)

Opened in 1908, the works closed in 1999 after its working life was extended by demand for cement to build the Channel Tunnel. The tunnel's boring machine was also tested here. After 0.9 mile / 1.4 kms you will reach the entrance to Oakley Hill nature reserve. Here you can walk alongside the quarry for a better view and also explore the reserve that is made up of old chalk downland, scrub and beech. It is a haven for wildflowers, particularly the Chiltern Gentian, and butterflies.

After returning to the entrance, turn left and go uphill along the side of the reserve. This path climbs very steeply until you reach and follow a fence to the road. Turn left, walking the short distance to Drifts where you go right on a footpath signed 'Sprigg's Alley ½'.

Now go ¼ right over the field. You will reach, enter and turn left in Venus Wood. Emerging from the wood, go ¼ right and continue until just before a lane. Before reaching the lane go sharp left to the right of a decorative old milk churn belonging to Pond Farm. Just past some farm buildings, go through a wooden gate and follow the edge of the trees. Descend to bridleway CH42 coming in from the right but keep straight up the other side of the valley on CH31a through Sunley Wood.

Again this is a steep uphill section. Follow the bridleway arrows and, when the path levels out and you reach the road to Chinnor, turn left and continue for about 500 yds / 450 mtrs until turning right onto Hill Top Lane. You will pass some inappropriate large houses on the way to the small car park at Chinnor Hill Nature Reserve (3).

In the reserve you will find a mixture of oak, ash and beech woodland and chalk grassland containing a great variety of wildflowers including several species of orchid. There are also ancient tracks and two Bronze Age burial mounds.

From the car park, near the site of an Iron Age settlement, take the bridleway signed 'Chinnor Barrows 400m' through the reserve. After walking along a clear path in attractive woodland, go left through a large kissing gate and then bear right onto the 'Wildlife Walk'.

There is now a superb view over Chinnor and Aylesbury Vale. Also nearby are the two Bronze Age barrows dating from 4600 – 3600BC.

Continue and go through another kissing gate and left downhill following a fence, passing chalk pits on your left. It is easier to take the embankment rather than the sunken path. Above, but hidden from view, is Bledlow Cross. At the bottom of the hill you reach and turn right onto The Ridgeway / Icknield Way at Point B.

Long and Short Walk from Point B

Keep on The Ridgeway, ignoring both a bridleway off to the left and the 'Swan's Way' as you pass a cottage. The Ridgeway now ambles very pleasantly through trees with fine views to the left. You slowly climb uphill before reaching and turning left onto a bridleway.

(If you turn right instead left and walk uphill for 400 yds / 365 mtrs, you can visit the Bledlow Cop. This is another burial mound, probably Bronze Age or possibly Saxon.)

Continue along the bridleway until reaching The Lions of Bledlow or, if you are a Midsomer Murders' fan, the Queen's Arms (PH). (Ignore a sign for Chinnor Reserve and Barrows on the way).

This is a rambling 16th century pub in a lovely setting that was originally the Blue Lion and Red Lion, hence the name. From the pub entrance, turn left and take the footpath with the cricket ground on your right.

When you reach a track (Swan's Way) bear right and continue until the track starts to go more steeply uphill (to the cottage you passed earlier). Here, opposite a 5bar gate, turn ½ right over a field, heading straight for a telegraph pole. Ignore a path that goes left, go forward and cross a stile. You now go between two fences and onward between a barn and a cottage to a 5bar gate with a thatched cottage, imaginatively called Thatched Cottage, ahead of you.

Turn right, and quickly left marked 'Chinnor ½'. Just before Chinnor the path meets a bridleway going right to the town, but you go left marked 'Ridgeway & Chinnor Reserve & Barrows'.

When you reach The Ridgeway turn right until you reach Hill Road. Now turn right downhill, cross to the footpath and you get to the narrow gauge railway on your left.

Starting Point: Station Entrance

SP757005
Explorer Map 171
Chiltern Hills West

Length:

Long Walk: 7 miles / 11.4 kilometres
Short Walk: 4 miles / 6.7 kilometres

Terrain:

The long version is quite demanding with very steep inclines. For a Sunday afternoon jaunt, the short level walk will be a better option.

Cholesbury

Iron Age Fort,
12th Century Manor, Highest Chilterns' Pub

Cholesbury Camp

Cholesbury Camp is an Iron Age fort covering approximately 15 acres / 6 ha. There are two banks that enclose the large ditch and when occupied there would have been wooden posts along the whole circumference of the inner bank and tree trunks supporting the walls. Excavations in the 1930s uncovered hearths and a clay oven with evidence of iron smelting. In the middle of the fort is St Lawrence Church. Built in the midst of a very poor community in 1220, there are no grand monuments and the parish was declared bankrupt in 1832. Due mainly to the efforts of long standing incumbent Henry Jeston, the church was rescued from financial ruin and restored in 1872.

From Parrott's Lane go through wooden gates, donated by local people in memory of villagers who died in the Great War, towards the church and quickly left onto the ditch that surrounded the fort (1).

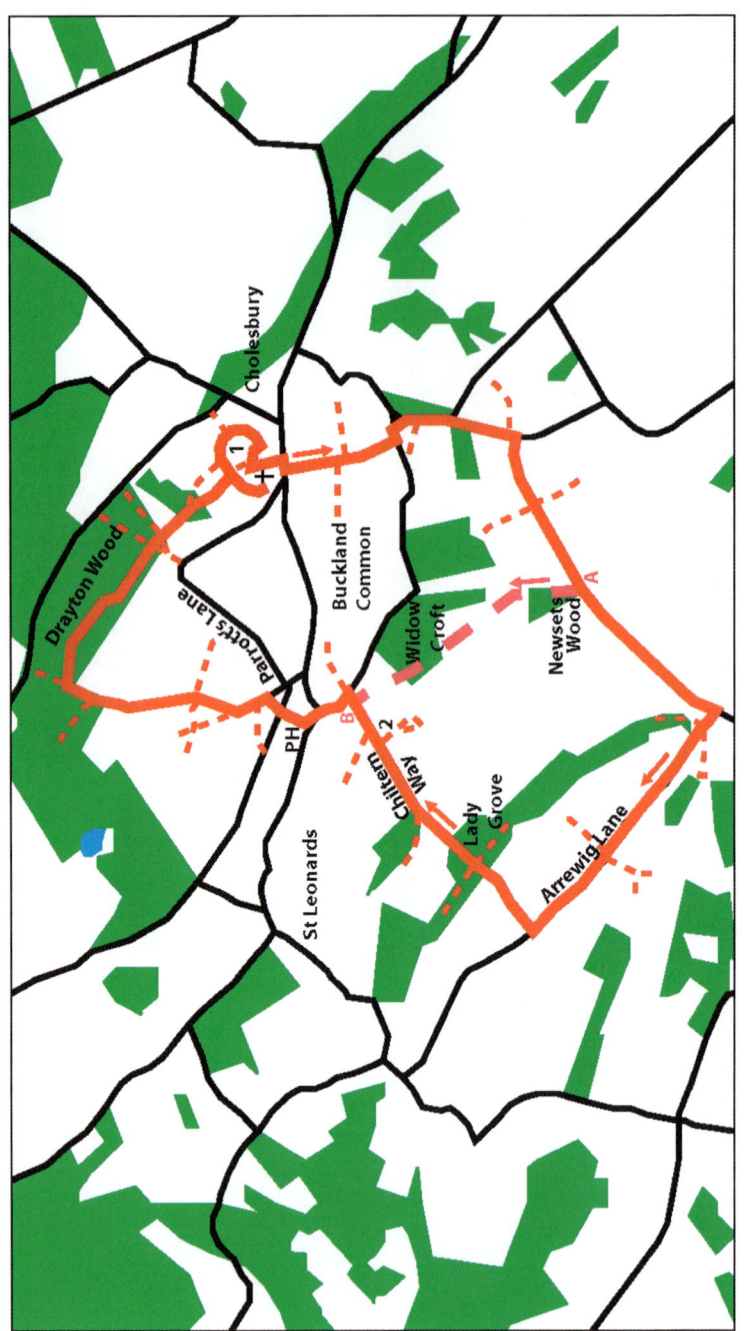

When you reach a crossing footpath, descend to the ditch. At about ¾ around the circumference you should glimpse a white house through a gap on the left. Here climb up onto the embankment on the right and follow a narrow path that will reach a stile. Cross the stile, go left to another and then, keeping to the left of the field past an old wooden barn with the church in view, you will turn left through a kissing gate next to a 5bar gate.

This path goes to the side of the Village Hall and you turn right onto the road. After a short distance turn left on a path that goes between The Old Rectory and Home Farm Cottage to a kissing gate.

You now head downhill to another kissing gate. Continue straight on up the other side of the valley (you may be able to see the top of a windmill on your left) to a further kissing gate and then an old metal gate next to a barn. Follow the track past the farmyard, through a five bar gate and onto a concrete drive to Oak Lane. Turn left.

Bear right at the road junction (marked Asheridge, Bellingdon and Chesham), and you reach a further junction just past Little Braziers Farm where you fork right (again to Asheridge). When you reach Cherry Tree Farm turn right onto a bridleway. Go through a gate and then ¼ left to the next one. Now keep straight across the field, through the boundary hedge (ignoring a crossing path) and onto the following field where you keep to the hedge on your left.

This sometimes muddy track reaches the edge of Newsets Wood at the corner of four fields. Continue straight on into the next field adjacent to the wood. After about 30 yds / mtrs the trees on your right end and there is a footpath going into the wood. This is Point A.

Short Walk from Point A

For the short walk turn right into Newsets Wood and follow the clear narrow path. When you reach the open go ¼ left over the field to a stile. The path bears left and then heads through a plantation. After continuing along a wire fence you enter Widow Croft.

35

The path now goes along the edge of the trees, then follows a hedge and finally the Dundridge Manor moat. Continue up to the manor's drive and turn right at Point B.

The long walk goes straight past Newsets Wood. Follow the track through a field boundary, and continue downhill, ignoring tracks that go off to the right and, further on, another that goes through the hedge.

At the valley bottom, go left though the hedge and there is a short climb and descent to Arrewig Lane. Turn right onto the Lane, along which you will now walk for ¾ mile / 1.2 km.

Ignore the footpath next to Arrewig Farm, carry on for a further 550 yds / 500 mtrs until you pass Autumn Cottage Farm and two home made 'Danger Slow' signs. A little further on turn right onto the Chiltern Way.

You now cross a field with an old pit in the middle and enter Lady Grove. Keep straight on the Chiltern Way and when you reach the open go ¼ right to a grass path that, after joining a bridleway, goes uphill to a concrete drive. Continue straight on and Dundridge Manor (2) will be on your right.

Although dating from c.1100, the Grade II listed house you can only just see today is largely 16th and 17th century. The moat, to protect cattle from thieves, is still visible and encloses about 4 acres / 1.4 ha of land. Timbers and other parts from the original house are still present although the drawbridge is 20th century.

Go through a double 5bar gate. Ignore a path to the left and continue along the drive, edged by snowdrops and daffodils in the spring.

You reach Point B when a footpath joins the drive from the right.

Long and Short Walk from Point B

At the end of the drive, turn left onto the lane and left again at a road junction to The White Lion (PH), tucked away on a bend in the road, it is the highest pub in the Chilterns and purveyor of a fine range of ever changing ales.

Take the path at the far side of the car park that dips to a lane (Bottom Road) and continue ¼ right across the next field to Little Twye Road. There is now a choice of routes back to the fort. Either, go right here and then left to follow Parrott's Lane all the way back.

Or, turn left on Little Twye Road (also the Chiltern Way). This is a road to nowhere and so very quiet. When the tarmac finishes, continue uphill on the shaded bridleway until the field on your right ends and you take a footpath off to the right into Drayton Wood.

The path follows the edge of the wood. You will reach one crossing path after approximately 800 yds / 730 mtrs. Ignore that one but turn right when you reach the next, go through a metal kissing gate and then over a stile into trees. After the wood ends, the path goes through a patch of brambles and then onward to the hill fort. Turn right along the ditch to return to the church entrance.

Starting Point: Entrance to St Lawrence Church

SP929071
Explorer Map 181
Chiltern Hills North

Length:

Long Walk: 5½ miles / 9 kilometres
Short Walk: 4¼ miles / 6.8 kilometres

Terrain:

An undulating walk with a mixture of farmland and woods.

Coombe Hill

Chilterns' Highest Viewpoint, Chequers, Iron Age Fort, Whiteleaf Cross, Nature Reserve

Coombe Hill Monument

Coombe Hill is the highest viewpoint in the Chilterns at 852 ft / 260 mtrs with marvellous views over the Vale of Aylesbury. The 106 acre / 43 ha area around Coombe Hill was once part of the Chequers estate but was given to the National Trust in the 1920s. The monument commemorates the 148 Buckinghamshire men who died in the Second Boar War and was erected in 1904 (rebuilt in 1938 after being destroyed by lightning).

From the monument, you must take The Ridgeway (following the acorn signposts) away from the viewpoint, just below the brow of the hill, with Ellesborough golf course and the Butler's Cross – Chequers road below on your right.

This becomes a narrow path that bears left to a wheelchair friendly metal kissing gate. Follow The Ridgeway through the woods until you reach a lane. Turn right on what is still The Ridgeway. After about 125 yds / 115 mtrs turn left at Lodge Hill Game Farm.

39

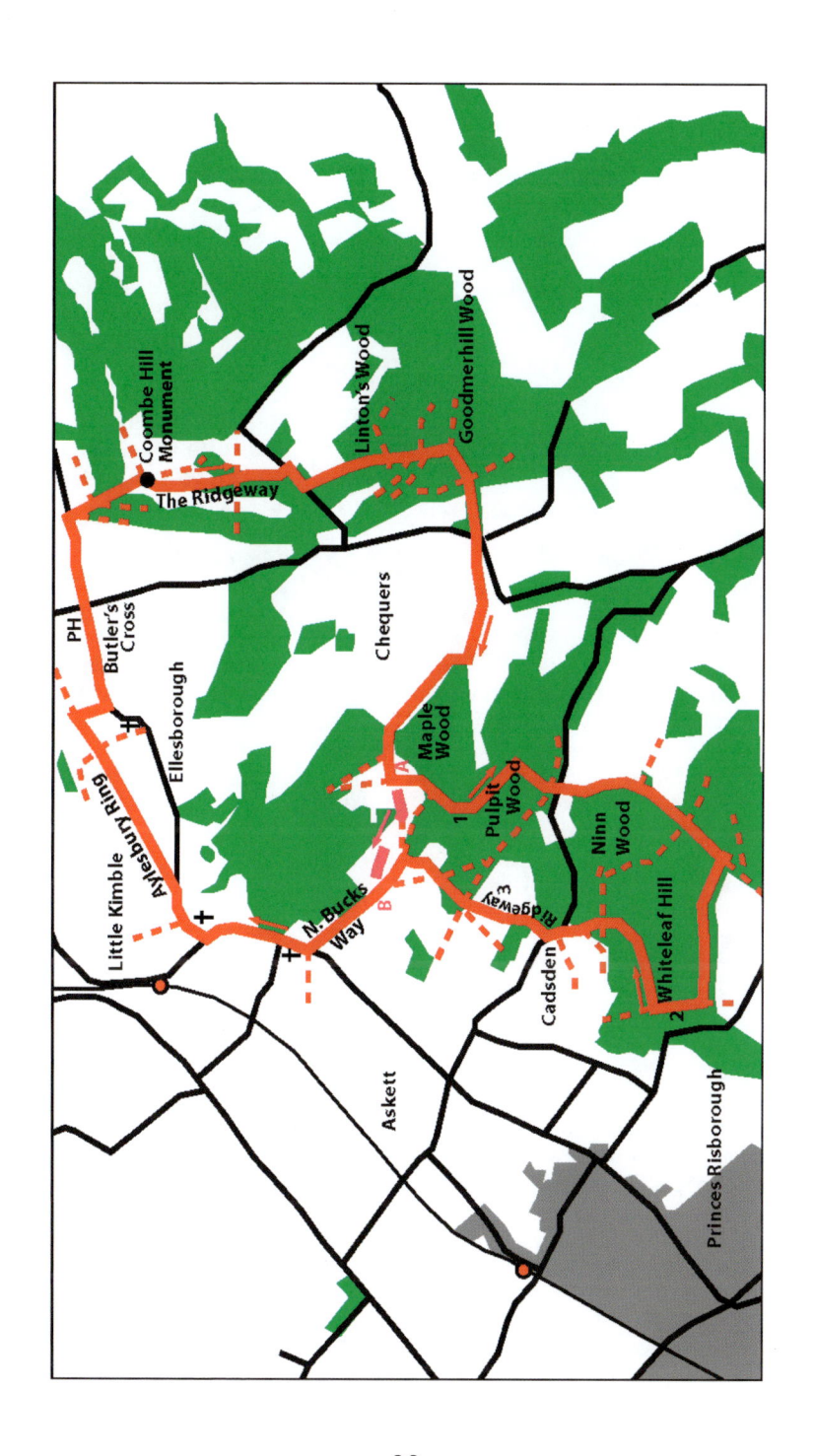

Take the concrete drive for a short distance before turning right over a stile. Now follow the footpath signs along the edge of the wood. The Ridgeway is well marked as it meanders through Linton's Wood and Goodmerhill Wood. Ignore any other footpaths and bridleways and eventually you will descend to the road to Great Missenden next to a row of houses.

Under the watchful eye of the CCTV cameras, cross the road and go through the small gate to the left of the five bar gate. Follow the clear path and cross a tarmac drive to head up to Maple Wood.

When you reach the trees turn right through a gate and follow the ugly metal fence with Chequers increasingly visible on your right. The house was given to the nation in 1917 and is the country residence of the Prime Minister.

At the gate at the end of the fence follow The Ridgeway sign ¼ right across the field. Point A is reached when you go through a metal kissing gate.

Short Walk from Point A

Keep on The Ridgeway along the 'Cradle Footpath' until taking the first footpath off to the right. The path soon divides, don't go downhill on the one that follows the edge of the field, fork left on the path that goes through a clump of trees and onward to an old metal kissing gate in the far corner of the field and turn right. This is Point B.

For the long walk, go through the kissing gate and then turn left leaving The Ridgeway. Just before a water trough go ½ right uphill. Once over a shallow ditch you will enter Maple Wood and reach a kissing gate. Go straight on, crossing a bridleway as you approach Pulpit Hill Fort (1).

Described by some as an unremarkable 4 acre / 1.6 ha Iron Age hill fort, I have always found it an impressive and evocative site. It follows the contours of the hill and has a single ditch and bank on the steep western sides, this is doubled on the east that is less easily defended. There are many other, probably Iron Age, earthworks in the woodland.

Look out for an arrowed tree and cross the fort diagonally. Once over a ditch on the other side of the fort, bear right and follow the same ditch and fence downhill to a wide track. Turn left onto the track.

When you reach a small Pulpit Hill direction sign turn right and descend quite steeply towards the road to Cadsden. Just before reaching a car park turn left along a bridleway. Then cross the road to the Icknield Way Riders Route opposite.

The track follows the edge of Ninn Wood. Ignore paths off to the left and right, and just after ½ mile / 0.8 km you will twist right and then quickly left. Ignore a permissive path to the right, and take the next footpath. This cuts a corner and you will turn right at the end rejoining the Riders Route.

This continues along the edge of the wood until reaching a well made track. Turn right here onto The Ridgeway leading to Whiteleaf Hill.

You will pass a neolithic barrow, circa 3700BC, and then catch a panoramic view of the surrounding countryside. Below is Whiteleaf Cross (2). Probably pre-1300s, nobody knows exactly when it was dug and why. It measures 79 ft / 24 mtrs wide and 85 ft / 26 mtrs high.

From the top of the hill take The Ridgeway through a wooden gate and then progress fairly steeply downhill. From painful personal experience this can be very slippery in wet weather, so watch your step.

Pass in front of The Plough at Cadsden and turn left along the main road, ignore the first path to the right, continue for a short distance and turn right following The Ridgeway.

After going through a gate and bearing left, The Ridgeway now goes through the Grangelands Nature Reserve (3) with its abundant fauna and flora including many orchids and butterflies. Cross a wide bridleway and proceed below Pulpit Hill.

You could go left and cut a corner but it is worth continuing along The Ridgeway past the 'rifle butts' on your right, formerly a shooting range.

You then climb some steps up to a wooden kissing gate and turn left on the North Bucks Way (Wolverton is only 35 miles if you fancy it). After just under 200 yds / 180 mtrs you reach Point B.

Long and Short Walk from Point B

Continue along the North Bucks Way until you reach Aylesbury Road. Turn right signposted 'Little Kimble 100m' and you get to St Nicholas Church at Great Kimble. It was here in 1635 that John Hampden held a meeting that led to his and others' refusal to pay Ship Tax and eventually the Civil War.

The Bernard Arms (closed at the time of writing) is a bit further on. Due to its proximity to Chequers, patrons included world leaders such as Boris Yeltsin. From The Bernard Arms go a short distance downhill, crossing over the road to take Ellesborough Road and reaching Little Kimble church.

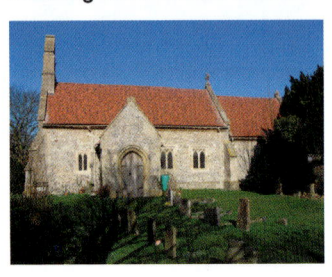

All Saints is renowned for its 14th century wall paintings, reputedly the finest in the county.

Continue along Ellesborough Road ignoring the first footpath on the left but taking the second through a front garden, marked 'Aylesbury Ring', just before a bus stop. You then go down an alley that leads to open fields with Beacon Hill and Ellesborough church shortly visible high on your right.

When you're directly below the church you could take the path up to it to enjoy a cup of tea and climb the tower on a summer Sunday afternoon or Bank Holiday.

If not, continue straight on the Aylesbury Ring until you reach a tarmac road at Springs Cottage. The lane will go right at Springs Farm, but you keep straight, taking the grass path to the left of a house. Continue until you get to Chalkshire Road and turn right.

At the end of Chalkshire Road is The Russell Arms (PH). This is a family and dog friendly pub that was saved by community action when under threat of closure.

Refreshment here will gird your loins for the forthcoming excursion to the top of Coombe Hill. From the pub turn left onto the Wendover Road. There is a proper footpath part of the way, then you have to walk on the road and turn right opposite the entrance to Ellesborough Golf Club.

On your right you will see the golf course. Once part of the Chequers estate, each Prime Minister since Lloyd-George has had honorary membership and it was a favourite place to play for Denis and Bill Deedes in the Thatcher years.

Don't take the bridleway on the left, keep on for a few yards through a gate and fork left on a signposted path uphill past a National Trust Coombe Hill sign. This is an extremely steep climb, ignoring a crossing footpath, up to the monument. It is not for anyone who is the least unfit.

Starting Point: Coombe Hill Monument

SP848067
Explorer Map 181
Chiltern Hills North

Length:

Long Walk: 7¾ miles / 12.59 kilometres
Short Walk: 5½ miles / 8.17 kilometres

Terrain:

Lots of fine autumn colour but beware the very steep climb up to the Coombe Hill monument, it literally isn't for the faint-hearted.

Ewelme

Water Cress Beds, Author's Grave, Two Historic Churches

Ewelme Water Cress Beds

The Ewelme water cress beds are one of the many success stories for the Chiltern Society. Established in the late 18th century, the chalk stream running through the village was dammed and widened to form a slow running, shallow body of water suitable for cress production. After ceasing commercial trading in 1988 the site was prevented from deteriorating by local effort but proper restoration only began after the beds were purchased by the society in 2000.

There is now a visitor centre and the adjoining wetlands boast a rich diversity of wildlife. From the Visitor Centre (1) follow the stream up High Street.

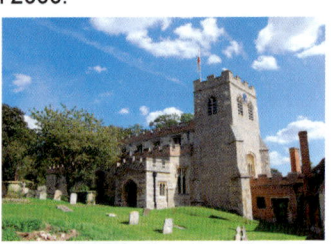

By going left just after the village hall you follow Parsons Lane to St Mary's Church. Built c.1430 and almost as the builders left it, it is closely associated with the Chaucers.

45

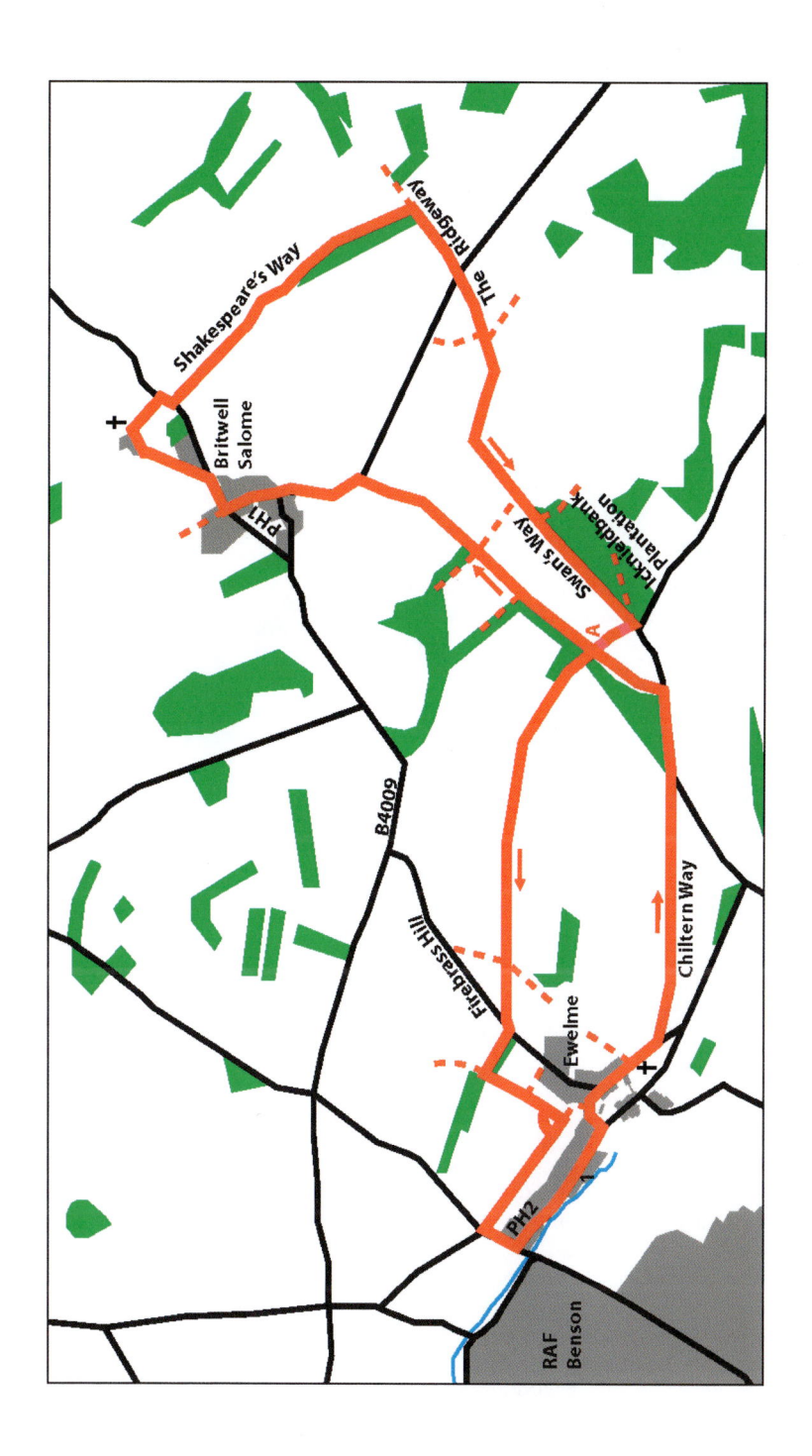

Look out for the tomb of Thomas Chaucer (son of Geoffrey the poet) and Alice, Duchess of Suffolk, the poet's granddaughter.

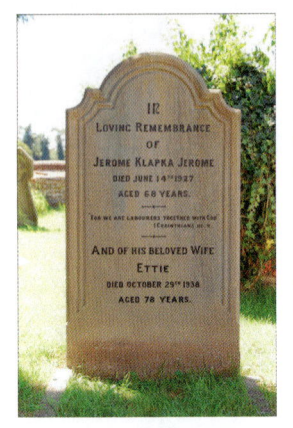

Attached to the church are almshouses and a school. The author of 'Three Men In A Boat', Jerome K. Jerome, is buried in the churchyard, a very different location from his Black Country birthplace for this Freeman of Walsall.

From the church turn right on Parsons Lane, away from the village, past the rectory and then fork left uphill on the Chiltern Way.

The track narrows to a path and, when you emerge into open countryside, go straight ahead along a wire fence with flat farmland to your left but glorious rolling hills on the right. After a short distance, look behind you for views of Didcot Power Station.

After dropping down to a lane, turn left following the Chiltern Way. Just after a plantation on your left take the bridleway marked 'Restricted Byway'.

When you reach the end of the plantation you will see a clear track in front of you in addition to a crossing track. This is Point A, where for a short walk you can turn left.

For the long walk, keeping straight on, you stay on this wide clear track. Ignore a path off to the left and a crossing path where the main track goes right, keep straight and you'll reach Monument Cottage and eventually a lane. Turn left and continue to a crossroads passing Foxington and its dovecot on the way.

Turn left to visit the village gastro pub (PH1), now called The Red Lion and getting very favourable reviews. If not, turn right. Ignoring the bridleway opposite, continue a short way looking out for a path on the left next to a road sign. Go ½ right (not over the cattle grid) keeping the fence / hedge on your right to a 5bar gate at the far end of the field.

Follow the lane to the left, past the pond and up to the church of St Nicholas, Britwell Salome. This quietly situated church dates from the 13th century but the very old churchyard yew suggests that it is predated by a much older structure. The surprisingly modern organ comes from Stokenchurch Methodist church.

Leaving through the main gate, turn left past the Old Rectory and through a 5bar gate marked Castle Hill in horseshoes next to a cattle grid.

When the track turns right up to stables, keep straight on to a stile onto the road from Watlington. Turn right and quickly left at Cooper's Farm. Continue straight through a long shaded section that narrows to a path before reaching The Ridgeway after just over ¾ mile / 1.2 kms.

Turn right onto The Ridgeway. You will cross a lane on this wide track and, when The Ridgeway goes left 350 yds / 300 mtrs from the lane, you keep straight onto the Swan's Way.

After a further 800 yds / 730 mtrs the wide track goes right but you keep straight on through Icknieldbank Plantation.

When you reach a car parking area turn right, returning to Point A (on the Chiltern Way). On the long walk when you reach Point A, keep straight on.

Long and Short Walk from Point A

The track rises by converted and existing barns and then heads in the direction of Didcot Power Station. The main track goes right 700 yds / 640 mtrs from the barns, but you keep straight along a narrow path and eventually, after a crossing path, you head uphill through elder and hawthorn bushes.

On reaching Firebrass Hill turn left and quickly right. In the autumn you can collect damsons on this restricted byway that's blocked by a large tree trunk.

When it ends turn left and keep straight with a large hedge on your right, parallel with Firebrass Hill on your left.

When you reach a 5bar gate turn right onto a permissive footpath. This arcs and joins a bridleway where you turn right. (Alternatively, continue straight from the 5bar gate, passing converted barns and turn right at The Hyde on the narrow bridleway).

At the end of the bridleway turn left onto a lane with RAF Benson just visible in front of you on the right. Go past Eyres Close and you reach the Shepherds Hut (PH2) and the water cress beds.

Starting Point: Watercress Beds Visitor Centre

SU641916
Explorer Map 171
Chiltern Hills West

Length:

Long Walk: 7¾ miles / 12.47 kilometres
Short Walk: 3¾ miles / 6.04 kilometres

Terrain:

These are easy undulating walks through attractive Oxfordshire farmland.

Great Missenden

Roald Dahl Museum and Story Centre, Liberty Figurehead, Balloon Club

Roald Dahl Story Centre

The writer Roald Dahl lived in Great Missenden for many years and in 2005 Cherie Blair officially opened the Museum and Story Centre that is based in an old coaching inn. It is a hive of Dahlesque activity and a repository for some of his works and papers. In 2008 the museum won the 'Best Small Visitor Attraction' award.

From the museum (1) go left into Church Street and then onto Church Lane, over the bypass and up to the parish church where the great man is buried. To visit the grave, take the path that bends left above the cemetery towards a bench encircled tree, the plot is a few giant footsteps away.

Return to the church, take a rough track uphill, and then a narrow path with a handrail to Frith Hill. Cross to Frith Hill South Heath Leg and then, just before a road sign indicating the lane will bend right, you fork left.

50

When you reach Frith Hill Stables and the drive bends uphill, look out for the half hidden narrow path that goes straight on and follows a wooden fence along the edge of the stables and parade ring. Next you go through woodland on a clear and well marked path.

At the edge of the wood, go through a kissing gate and immediately go right. Proceed between wooden fences and then through a kissing gate. Keep straight, at first following the edge of the wood and then ¼ right across the field towards a row of pylons and another kissing gate.

Now follow a barbed wire fence under the pylons to a stile into trees, onto a path that goes ¼ left. On the other side of the wood, go straight over the field to the lane from South Heath. This is Point A.

Short Walk from Point A

Turn left onto the lane and walk 600 yds / 550 mtrs to Point B, ignoring a footpath at Park Farm.

For the long walk, cross the lane following the 'Chiltern Heritage Trail' and go slightly left over the field to a stile next to a line of oak trees. The path goes through a hedge and follows the trees and then the edge of the field as it bends round under telegraph wires to a stile. Cross the stile and go left along a wooden fence. Look out for and take the first footpath on the left through a gap in the hedge, over a stile and then immediately right.

Follow the field edge and, just after the corner, you reach a gap in the hedge. Go over the stile, still following the heritage trail, along the hedge on your right to another stile and two 5bar gates.

Go to the left of a third gate and quickly turn left on a crossing path before the next stile. Follow the edge of the cricket field, turning right to go along the football pitch touchline.

At the lane turn left, pass the very small St. Mary's Church, and then continue straight on a hedge lined bridleway. This is a very pleasant 700 yds / 655 mtrs walk until you reach a bench, where you can have a rest and observe the odd Red Kite drifting by.

The track bears sharp right and widens. Continue past several houses and turn left onto a bridleway just before Croft Dell.

After 550 yds / 500 mtrs, just before the track becomes shaded and muddy, there are paths forking left and right, take the latter option and go along the edge of a paddock. Turn right on the lane to Pipers and the Liberty figurehead (2).

The chap starring at you is Earl Howe and the figurehead was taken from an eponymous ship, while the timbers were used on construction work at the Liberty's London store. The family still live at Pipers.

Retrace your steps to the bridleway, cross and now take the left fork. Follow the hedge on your left initially as it arcs but then cross the field along what is left of a field boundary hedge to a large cow shed on your right.

You will see a stile in the hedge next to the shed, don't cross it, go to the left of the hedge and follow the edge of the field to a stile next to a clump of trees.

Go straight over the next field to a white topped post and continue to the right of the hedge.

When you reach a stile go ½ right over the next field underneath a row of telegraph wires. Keep straight at the field boundary (i.e. diagonally across the next field) to a double stile, then go ½ right.

You will reach and turn right onto a lane from South Heath at Point B.

Long and Short Walk from Point B

Walk past a row of cottages, including one that presumably used to be The Lamb pub, and take the next footpath on your left. Keep to the left edge of this field and the next before going through a hedge.

Most people will now keep to the right side of this field, however, the official footpath crosses to the other side. Either way, you go through the next field boundary under a line of pylons. Now continue on the left side of another two fields to a stile overlooking Great Missenden.

Now bear ½ left as the path heads just to the left of a distant block of flats in Great Missenden. When you reach the main road, be careful as it is very busy, cross over and go right, parallel with the road at first, and then crossing the field to a kissing gate and onward to the ballooning club and Black Horse (PH).

From the pub, walk along the road to Great Missenden passing some quaint shops on the frequently traffic challenged High Street back to the museum.

Starting Point: Roald Dahl Story Centre

SP895012
Explorer Map 181
Chiltern Hills North

Length:

Long Walk: 6¼ miles / 10 kilometres
Short Walk: 3¾ miles / 6 kilometres

Terrain:

Not a particularly taxing, mainly farmland, walk - climbing at the start and then descending to Great Missenden to finish.

Hambleden

Winery and Brewery, Deer Park

Chiltern Valley Winery and Brewery

When the first grapes were harvested in 1984 at the Chiltern Valley Winery and Brewery, producing English wine was still considered by many to be an eccentric activity. Now vastly increased in popularity, 120,000 bottles of award winning wine are turned out annually in addition to bottled and cask real ale. Their shop is open seven days a week with tours and tastings taking place regularly. And if you feel like popping the question, you can also get married there!

From the main entrance (1), go uphill along the quiet lane for approximately 700 yds / 640 mtrs until turning left onto a footpath that crosses under a line of pylons and then into trees. Keep straight on when the track bears left and, when you reach the open, go right following the edge of the field until reaching an old broken 5bar gate next to a new one. Go through the old gate and ¼ left over the next field to a stile.

Cross a sunken bridleway (Shakespeare's Way) and follow the fenced off path that will go left to a stile, then towards farm buildings.

55

Go through a 5bar gate and then along an attractive drive lined by beech trees. You reach a lane and turn right. Go downhill for short distance and take a footpath on the left just before a white house. The path descends sharply, at the bottom cross a track and stile to ascend on path F8 following a line of telegraph poles. After reaching a stile, continue straight along a track to Bosmore Farm.

Proceed into the farm, with working barns and then the Estate Office on your right as you bear left to Bosmore Farm Barns. Go to the left of these converted barns and then follow the lane behind them.

You then pass Bosmore Farmhouse and a pond before reaching the gates of a very large house indeed (Bosmore Park). Just after this house turn left through a gate into a mixed plantation (Annabelle's Wood).

At the far end of the wood, go through a gate and head for the white house directly ahead. Then go ½ right at the next field boundary. At the far side of the field turn right onto a lane.

After a short distance turn left onto a bridleway marked 'Stonor ½'. After 200 yds / mtrs, before reaching a Stonor Estate sign, turn right on a narrow bridleway that follows a tall wire mesh fence steeply downhill to the B480. Turn right and, just before a cricket ground on the left, turn right again onto the Chiltern Way into Stonor Park.

Follow the Chiltern Way through the park, with marvellous views over the surrounding countryside, perhaps catching sight of the herd of fallow deer here since medieval times.

In the same family since 1150, the house was built between the 12th and 16th centuries and has an outstanding collection of paintings and tapestries together with a library dating from the 1600s. There is also a 14th century chapel and, interestingly for a location with such strong Catholic connexions, a reconstructed stone circle.

Once past the house, when the wide track bears right uphill, keep straight on a narrow path to the left of a fence, with the old stables below. On leaving the park through a gate, you emerge into an attractively shrubbed valley and climb steadily following arrows to a lane. This is Point A.

Short Walk from Point A

For the short walk back to the vineyard, keep straight over the lane onto a track that passes Kiln Cottage. Then go over a stile next to a 5bar gate and keep straight for about 30 yds / mtrs before taking a stile on your right. Turn left, you will notice that this is the Shakespeare's Way, go along the edge of the field past a fenced off pit until you reach another stile. Cross the stile and go right following the hedge until you reach a stile at the bottom of the field into Gussetts Wood. Go downhill, cross a bridleway and continue straight uphill when the clear path will wind up to another stile.

Now proceed ¼ left over a field and, leaving the Shakespeare's Way, turn left onto the lane back to the vineyard.

For the long walk, follow the Chiltern Way left and then right at Southend onto a lane that is initially concrete and then turns to tarmac.

Walk along this pleasant lane until you reach The American Barn, then continue along the Chiltern Way through horse country. Descending, with Cobstone Mill directly in front on top of the hill, you will reach and turn right on Dolesden Lane. Ignore the bridleway that goes right, continue and turn right onto the next footpath that passes a gas installation and, when you reach open ground, go ¾ right.

Once inside the trees again, follow the track uphill through Poynatts Wood. Normally a path such as this one might be a nightmare to follow with tracks that leave on the left and right but this is exceptionally well marked. When the track bends left and forks, take the left option and after descending go left again (clearly arrowed).

The track eventually narrows to a path and descends to the lane leading into Skirmett. Here go left to the pub or right to the vineyard. The Frog (PH) is an attractive place that like many country establishments has had to re-invent itself as an eating place / conference centre / B&B to survive but the public bar is well worth visiting.

To return to the vineyard, leave Skirmett along the lane in the direction of Hambleden and turn right on the first footpath next to a 'Beware of Deer' sign.

58

Follow the barbed wire posts up to the trees, go right and, after a short distance, left up a steep incline. When you reach the edge of the wood go ½ right over a field towards the vineyard and then follow the footpath to the lane that goes up to the front entrance.

Starting Point: Chiltern Valley Winery and Brewery (Luxters Farm)

SU768890
Explorer Map 171
Chiltern Hills West

Length:

Long Walk: 7½ miles / 12 kilometres
Short Walk: 6 miles / 9.6 kilometres

Terrain:

Plenty of woodland with several testing hills for those not used to the Chilterns and a surprising number of stiles.

Ivinghoe

Britain's Oldest Post Mill, Ivinghoe Beacon, Ford End Water Mill

Pitstone Mill

Pitstone Mill stands just outside Ivinghoe. It claims to be the oldest post mill in Britain possibly dating from 1627. Badly damaged in 1902, the National Trust took it over in the 1930s. It is open to the public on summer Sundays.

From the car park on the B488, cross the road, turning left towards Ivinghoe. Turn right on the first footpath you come to (signposted Ivinghoe Beacon) and follow a clear path along the field edge, initially to the left and then switching to the right of a hedge.

When the hedge ends, continue straight across open ground. The path then bears left past an embankment and onto a stile. Continue ¼ left slightly uphill until you reach a lonely hawthorn bush with Incombe Hole in front of you.

60

61

Resist the temptation to take the wide path you can see around the rim of the Hole. Instead bear right and you will quickly see and then reach a sign post. Turn left at the post and follow The Ridgeway as it winds uphill with Incombe Hole on your left.

You eventually reach a stile and gate (just past a path that goes right to another stile).

Go to the left of the gate and stile, following the acorn sign up to a spinney of hawthorn bushes.

Follow the clear path out of the wood. Ignore the first stile on the right, follow the fence downhill and turn right through the next kissing gate marked The Ridgeway. Continue on the path to Beacon Road.

When you reach the road, cross it and follow the signs and wide chalk track to Ivinghoe Beacon. Given to the National Trust in the 1920s, this is where The Ridgeway starts on its way to Avebury and is 800 ft / 245 mtrs above sea level. It is the site of an ancient hill fort covering 5 acres / 2 ha and is adjacent to several Bronze Age burial mounds.

From the beacon follow an extremely steep path (if you are looking at the map display at the top of the beacon, this path is on your left) downhill to the road that you crossed to reach the beacon, just before a cattle grid and the junction with the A489. There are easier ways to descend but this is the quickest.

At the junction turn right and quickly left through a kissing gate onto the Two Ridges Link. Follow the fence along the field edge passing another kissing gate. Further on, after a telegraph pole set in the fence, look out for a sign nailed onto the fence, just before a hedge laden with elderberries in the autumn begins. Here turn right heading straight towards Edlesborough church in the distance.

Just before reaching the lane that leads into Ivinghoe Aston, turn left through a kissing gate and follow the path above the lane. At the field corner go through the hedge onto the lane.

Going through Ivinghoe Aston, you will have no difficulty finding The Village Swan (PH), a pub thankfully saved from developers by the villagers. From the pub, walk through the village and once past Orchard Farm go left onto the first footpath you get to. Now go left and proceed along the edge of the field, bearing right at the corner to follow a stream on your left.

You now follow the hedge and the stream, that becomes a water filled ditch, over several field boundaries, including going over a footbridge through one hedge. After the path meets a crossing farm track with a 5bar gate and fence in front of you, go left, and then right on an improved surface.

Turn left (clearly marked just before you reach several barns and farm buildings) up to a golf course. Passing the golf course, you soon enter Ivinghoe via a small estate at the end of a narrow path.

Bear right, walking through the estate until you get to the main road. Here turn right to the Ford End Water Mill. On the site of an earlier structure, this one dates from the 1700s and has been restored to recreate an 1880s corn mill.

It is one of only a few in the country still working with the original machinery and stoneground flour can be purchased on Open Days.

Retrace your steps to Ivinghoe and you will reach St Mary's Church that dates from 1220 and was deliberately set on fire in 1234 to spite the local bishop. From the church go back to the car park, walking the short distance on the A488.

Starting Point: Pitstone Mill Car Park

SP946157
Explorer Map 181
Chiltern Hills North

Length:

5½ miles / 9 kilometres

Terrain:

Outstanding views but to reach them there are demanding ascents and one particularly steep downhill section.

Jordans

Quaker Estate, Captain Cook Memorial, Milton's Cottage

Friends' Meeting House

Jordans is a 20th century estate that has its origins in the 1600s. The Meeting House was constructed by local Quakers, including William Penn (of Pennsylvania fame) and Thomas Ellwood (see John Milton), following the 1688 Toleration Act that gave freedom to their form of worship.

Both men are buried here with family members including Gulielma Penn (see the Amersham walk). The house is open to visitors on certain days. There's a small lay-by for cars.

From the house (1) continue through the new part of the graveyard and take the path to the Mayflower Barn, traditionally supposed to have been built from the timbers of the ship that carried the Pilgrim Fathers to America in 1620. Next to it is Old Jordans - the original Quaker meeting place.

Walk a short distance up the road and turn left into the Jordans estate.

66

The estate was built on land acquired by the Quakers in 1919. Completed in 1923, the community is still run on Quaker principles.

Walk straight across the top of the village green and downhill over Copse Lane into a cul de sac. Then turn right on a crossing bridleway. After passing some rather impressive houses you reach and turn left on Twitchells Lane and then, after 200 yds / mtrs, go left on a footpath that is a concrete drive.

When the track bends sharply, keep straight, over a stile through a hedge and then along the right edge of the field, under a row of pylons to a kissing gate. Proceed over a crossing path and continue along a wooden fence to Willow Court Stables and Newbarn Lane.

Turn left onto the lane and when it turns sharply left keep straight onto Rawlings Lane, turning immediately right into New Barn Farm and quickly going to the left of a hedge. This path is narrow and somewhat overgrown. Bear right over a stile, continuing along a narrow path through trees. Go over a crossing path and another track, until you reach a stake, where you go ¼ left over the adjacent field.

Once into Hodgemoor Woods be careful to take the well worn path just inside the edge of the trees that runs parallel with the bridleway on the outside edge of the wood.

After a wire fence, go straight onto a riders trail (Spring Link). Fork left before getting to a wooden horse barrier and go uphill to Botterells Lane that is just after a crossing trail. Turn right, go around one corner but keep straight at the next one onto the Chiltern Way. When you reach Hill Farm House there is a helpful road sign as you continue towards London Road on the Chiltern Way past the old stables and dairy. The path goes downhill and crosses to the other side of the hedge. Now follow the wire fence downhill to a kissing gate.

Turn right, on the Chiltern Way. You'll reach a lane, go left and quickly right, and eventually pass some imposing houses on your way to Chalfont St Giles. Across the green is Merlin's Cave (PH), noted for its jazz on Sunday lunchtimes and well worth patronising before or after visiting The Vache.

To visit The Vache (Captain Cook) Memorial:

Bearing in mind that the memorial isn't publicised and the footpath can be 'restricted or withdrawn at any time', leave Chalfont St Giles, going uphill to the junction with the A413. Cross and continue up Vache Lane for about 600 yds / 550 mtrs until you reach, on the left, a private drive leading to Vache Mews and Vache Lodge.

Walk along the tarmac drive and you will begin to pass manicured lawns with large houses. Just by a pair of white gates before Garden Cottage you'll see a sign pointing the way along a narrow path. After 270 yds / 250 mtrs you reach the monument. It was built by the retired Admiral Sir Hugh Palliser, Captain Cook's friend and patron, who lived at The Vache.

After reading about the exploits of 'the ablest and most renowned Navigator this or any other country has produced', who rose 'from very obscure birth to the rank of Post Captain in the royal navy', you may climb the stairs for a view of the surrounding estate. You are allowed to visit the monument through the largesse of the Russian family who now own The Vache and refurbished the monument in 2007, and the hard work of the Chiltern Society establishing access.

After retracing your steps, walk straight through Chalfont St Giles. The village might seem familiar as it doubled as Walmington-on-Sea in the 1971 Dad's Army film and has appeared in other productions requiring the backdrop of 'Britain's Most Perfect Village'. After passing Merlin's Cave, The Crown and The Feathers, you reach Milton's Cottage (2), open daily except Mondays during the summer.

It was here that Milton completed his masterpiece Paradise Lost. The cottage was secured for John Milton and his family by his friend Thomas Ellwood when he fled the plague in 1665. It has been preserved since 1887 and houses the world's finest collection of his first editions.

From the museum continue uphill and take the first footpath on the left just before Hillside Close. The path will bend sharp right to a football pitch and then left parallel to Bowstridge Lane. You pass a playground and then a cricket pitch followed by a bowling club. Continue straight along the edge of the field across a bridleway and onward past some horse paddocks. Go along this narrow path until you reach Narcot Lane at the end of a wire mesh fence. Cross straight over.

At the first direction stake, turn right along a shaded path between two fields. At the next turn left. Then straight on at a further stake and continue, going through a metal kissing gate, until turning left on a crossing path over a stile under a row of pylons. Now follow the pylons through kissing gates before going ½ left under them.

Turn right along a tarmac drive for 600 yds / 550 mtrs to Welders Lane, where you turn right and walk 925 yds / 845 mtrs to return to the Friends' Meeting House.

Starting Point: Friends' Meeting House

SU974910
Explorer Map 172
Chiltern Hills East

Length:

7¼ miles / 11.7 kilometres
(9¼ mls / 14.9 kms inc. The Vache)

Terrain:

Mostly what can be referred to as urban farmland including a seemingly endless succession of horse paddocks.

Lacey Green

Rupert Brooke's Local, Lacey Green Windmill, John Hampden Monument and Grave

> If I should die, think only this of me:
> That there's some corner of a foreign field
> That is forever England.

This was Rupert Brooke as war poet, three well known lines from one of the small number of sonnets that earned him a reputation rivalling such heavyweights as Wilfred Owen and Siegfried Sassoon. Before the war he had been the 'handsomest man in England' eulogising with a friend, Jacques Raverat, about fine times spent in this isolated pub in the Chilterns -

> Never came there to the Pink
> Two such men as we, I think
> Never came there to the Lily
> Two men quite so richly silly

Warwickshire born in 1887, he died on a Greek island in 1915, not surviving long enough to adopt the cynicism of his peers in the trenches. He loved the Chilterns where he 'walked so far' and the 'Pink' in which he 'sang so loud'.

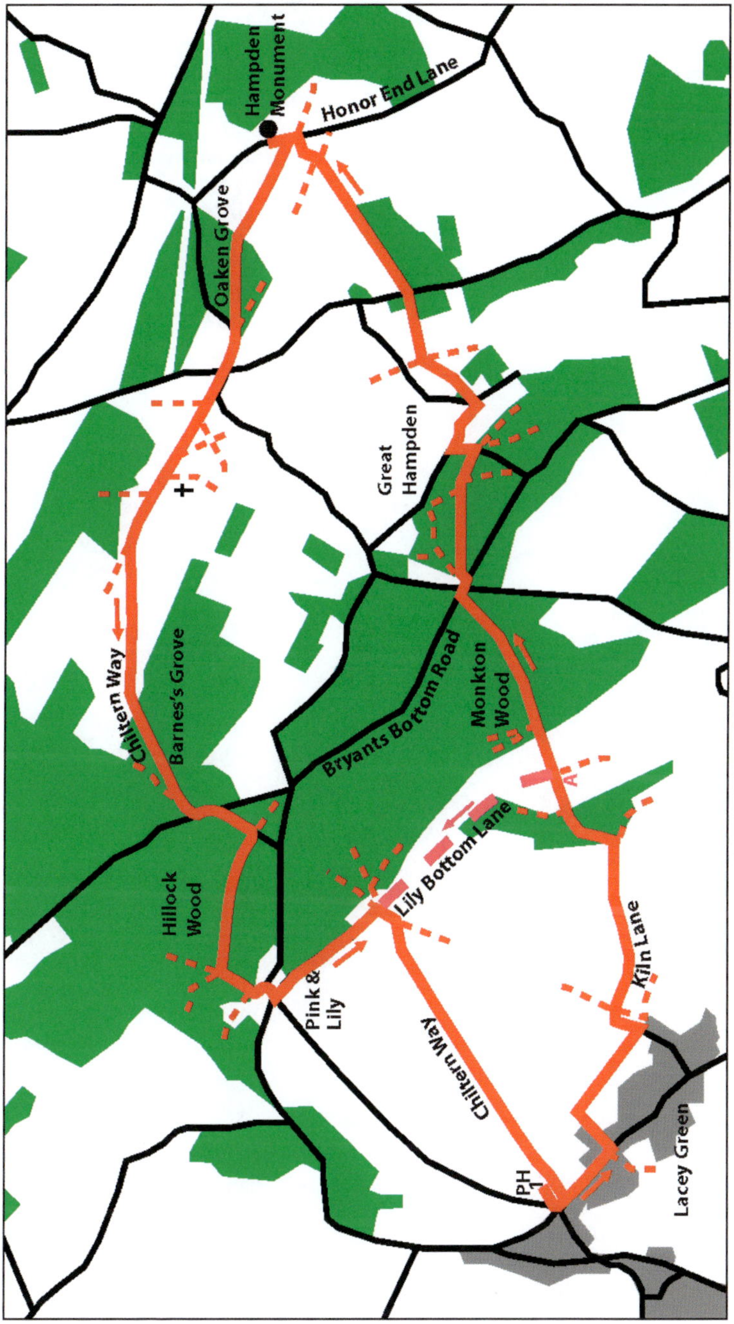
Hampden Monument
Honor End Lane
Oaken Grove
Great Hampden
Chiltern Way
Barnes's Grove
Bryants Bottom Road
Monkton Wood
Hillock Wood
Lily Bottom Lane
Pink & Lily
Kiln Lane
Chiltern Way
PH
Lacey Green

The pub's unusual name is derived from Mr Pink, a butler at Hampden House, who established the hostelry in the 19th century with his partner Miss Lillie, a chambermaid.

Take Lily Bottom Lane at the side of the pub and just past Iron Beech Cottage go right onto the Chiltern Way alongside Lily Bank Farm. After climbing for a short distance look out for and take a footpath off to the right. Go ½ left over the field. From the next stile go ¼ right towards the far corner near a pylon.

You can now see Lacey Green Windmill (1) and follow the Chiltern Way arrows across several horse paddocks all the way to it.

This might be the oldest surviving smock mill in the country but it has occupied its current position only since 1821, having previously been sited in Chesham for 170 years. Restored by the Chiltern Society, it is open on Sunday afternoons during the summer and each May, on National Mills Day, the sails are cranked into action.

Next to the windmill is The Whip Inn (PH), a pub that boasts an unrivalled roster of real ales. From the Whip or the entrance to the windmill turn left along the Main Road, past the ornate bus stop.

Take the first road on the left, Goodacres Lane. Continue straight along a track and turn right just before a 5bar gate on an unmarked path through a small gate next to another 5bar gate and then along a hedge. After following the edge of the field, the path narrows with hedges each side. You then turn left down a bridleway that bears right and meets a crossing bridleway.

Continue along the wide track (Kiln Lane), ignoring a track that forks left, and passing Kingswood House. Then look out for and turn left on a bridleway that goes uphill along the edge of a wood. After ignoring a path to the left and getting to open ground, the path narrows and you will reach a Restricted Byway (Lily Bottom Lane). This is Point A.

Short Walk from Point A

To return to the Pink & Lily turn left on Lily Bottom Lane and continue all the way back to the pub.

On the long walk, cross the lane and go between a stretch of overgrown wooden fences. You then enter Monkton Wood. Here keep straight to the left of the fence where there is a footpath.

It can be a muddy slog but you will eventually reach Bryants Bottom Road. Turn right onto the road and quickly cross over to a wooden gate. Go immediately ½ right uphill through Hampden Coppice. Don't take the Permitted Footpath that forks right, continue and, when the path levels, ignore a crossing path and then descend to a road. Turn left onto the road and, after ignoring a footpath to Bryants Bottom, turn right at the subsequent road junction.

The lane winds uphill and gets to a junction where you take the footpath into the trees opposite. You will shortly be in the open and the path follows the edge of the field. When the hedge ends, go straight over the field between two old oaks. Instead of going left over the next field (following a path to a gap in the hedge next to a telegraph pole), bear right with a hedge on your right. You continue into trees and descend to a road.

Cross to the footpath opposite and, following arrows, bear left into a field. Now go right along the edge of this field and the next until you reach horse paddocks. Climb a stile and go between them towards Honor End Farm. At the farm cross over a stile onto a gravel drive to Honor End Lane and then left to the John Hampden Monument.

The monument was erected in 1863 to the memory of the man who refused to pay 'Ship Money' - as it was 'without authority of the law'.

John Hampden's refusal to pay the tax demanded by Charles I took place in 1635 and it was one in a series of events that culminated in the Civil War. After raising a militia he eventually died at the Battle of Chalgrove Field in Oxfordshire in 1643.

After visiting the monument, retrace your steps, go back along the gravel drive and climb the stile. Go straight on to a gate and the next stile. Bear right and follow the edge of the field with a hedge on your right across one field boundary and into Oaken Grove. Go ¼ left gently uphill on an initially narrow path until you reach a double 5bar gate and stile. Turn left onto the road that quickly bends right to a junction.

Follow the sign to Gt. Hampden and Speen. When the road bends left, continue straight through an electric gate to Great Hampden church.

St Mary Magdalen's interest lies in the fact that it is the last resting place of John Hampden. The exact location of his grave is unknown but there is a monument to his memory, erected by his great-grandson in 1743.

From the church, go past Turret House on the left and Hampden House on the right. The latter was formerly occupied by Hammer Films and was used frequently in their horror movies. Continue on the Chiltern Way through a 5bar gate. Walk along the track and go through a gate and then diagonally over the large field to a spinney in the middle, where there is a white topped post that isn't immediately apparent. You then continue in the same direction across the field to a small white post that again isn't very visible, at the edge of Barnes's Grove.

Going into the grove follow the marked trees ¼ right. You eventually meet another path coming in from the right and continue along Grim's Ditch to the road. Cross the road and follow the Chiltern Way along the lane in the direction of Lacey Green.

Turn right at the first footpath sign (adjacent to the last house) and go into Hillock Wood. Following a Purple Route sign, go ½ left. After 20 yds / mtrs look out for a small tree arrow, after a further 15 yds / mtrs go ½ right (not marked).

You will reach a stake and follow a purple marker across a track and along a wide straight path between the trees. Just past a disused style leave the Purple Route and turn left onto a crossing bridleway.

Go forward until bearing left at the gate of Hampden Lodge. Turn right onto the road to the Pink & Lily.

Starting Point: Pink & Lily

SP827018
Explorer Map 181
Chiltern Hills North

Length:

Long Walk: 7½ miles / 12.07 kilometres
Short Walk: 3½ miles / 5.63 kilometres

Terrain:

No serious hills and lots of woodland, excellent colour in the autumn.

Latimer & Chenies

A Horse's Grave, Chenies Manor

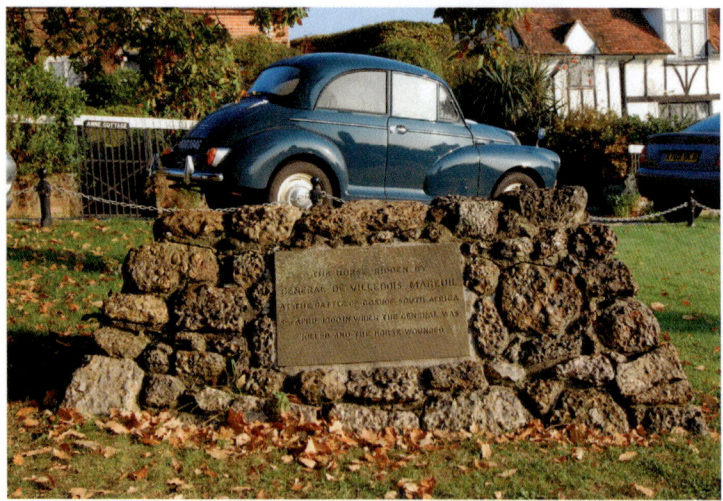

Latimer

Latimer is a quiet village on the road from Little Chalfont to Flaunden. The attractive green is surrounded by 17th and 18th century houses and has two memorials with a Boar War connexion - one is a traditional obelisk but the other is, rather unusually, the grave of a horse. The story is that the animal was injured in the Boar War while fighting under General de Villebois Maruil who was killed. Lord Chesham brought the horse back to England and it, or its heart, was ceremoniously buried on the green in 1911.

From the green (1) take the road towards Little Chalfont. Just after leaving the village turn left on the Chess Valley Walk. After going through a kissing gate, next to a sign warning that your dog may be shot, go forward past a small oak tree and under a row of telegraph wires. Then follow another line of telegraph poles along the top of the field to a metal gate next to a 5bar gate. On your right, completely overgrown and hidden from view, are the remains of the old Flaunden church of St Mary Magdalene. Old Flaunden suffered from constant flooding as it was on the banks of the River Chess, so the village moved uphill from Buckinghamshire into Hertfordshire during the early 1800s. There is a display board with details if you look hard enough.

Having gone through the gate, you will pass the 1777 grave of William Liberty, a local brickmaker and relative of the retailing Libertys.

77

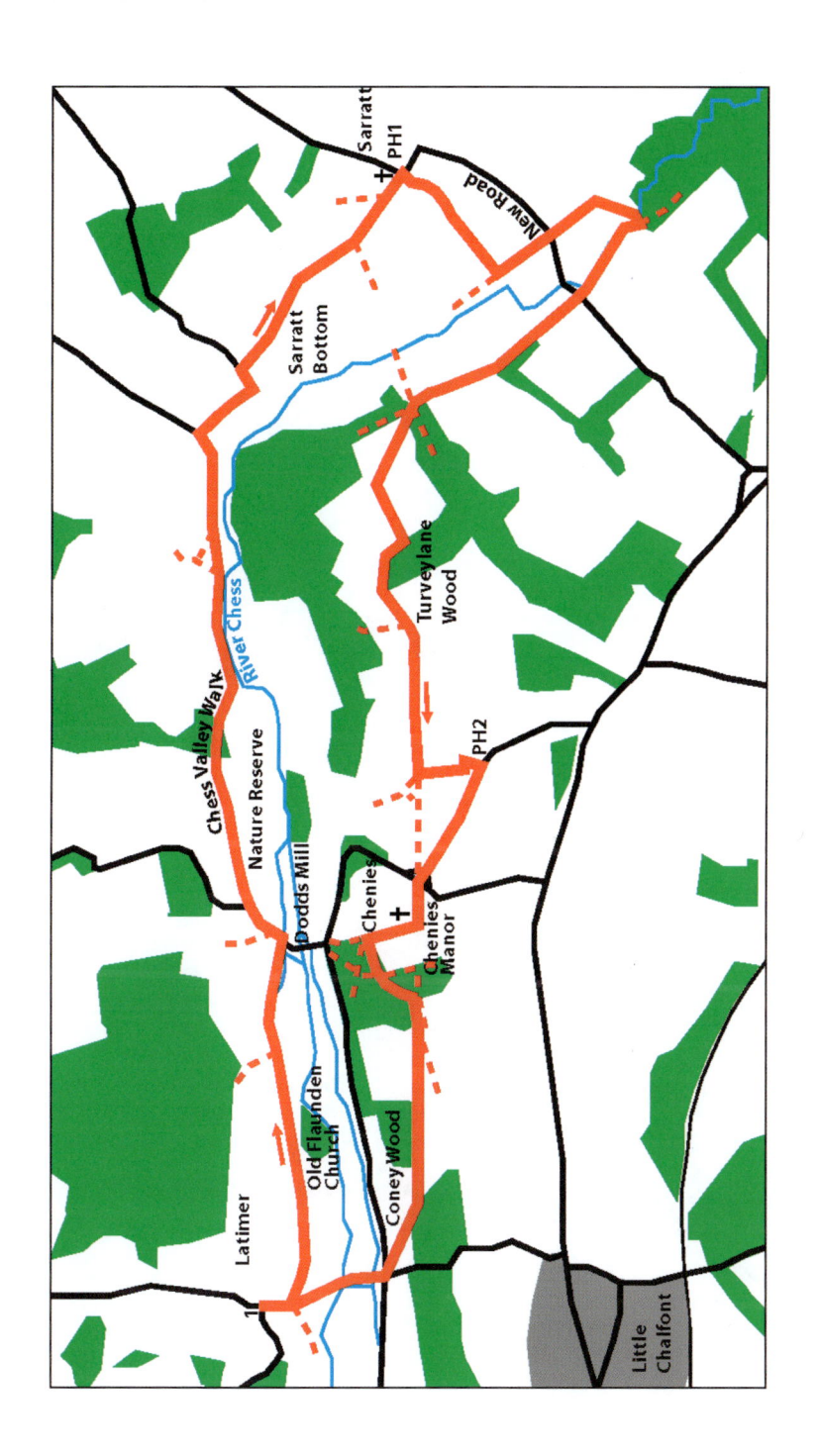

Go through another metal gate and keep straight, ignoring a bridleway and path going off to the left. Soon the path can resemble a tributary of the Chess, but the worst is over when you get to a wooden gate and continue through Mill Farm to the road.

(If you turn right here and go a short distance to opposite Dodds Mill, there is a great view of the river). From Mill Farm turn left along the road and follow the Chess Valley Walk that goes right through a metal gate after about 100 yds / mtrs.

Follow wooden fences past meadows that used to be deliberately flooded to aid soil fertility. After going through a wooden kissing gate continue past a mass of brambles, while looking out for the Frogmore Meadow Nature Reserve coming up on the right, a haven for water voles.

Go through a kissing gate into trees and follow the distinct path out of the wood and then between barbed wire fences.

Wooden slats will now punctuate the walk until you reach Valley Farm. Here you can go right to a ford with another attractive view of the Chess and, after reading about the history of local cress beds, buy fresh bunches from the last commercial producer in the Chilterns.

Continue along the concrete drive that goes in front of Valley Farm, following the river. At the end of the drive follow the Chess Valley Walk sign to the right. When you reach the half hidden sign for Sarratt Bottom, turn left up a lane passing Cakebread Cottage. Just past the cottage turn right to a kissing gate with a 'Sarratt ½' signpost.

Follow the hedge on your right and at the first stile go ¼ left over the next field to the far corner. Ignore a stile on your left and continue uphill along a barbed wire fence through an avenue of trees up to a 5bar gate and stile. Go over the stile and straight on following a row of holly bushes. At the end of the holly, go right to the Church of the Holy Cross, Sarratt. Following construction around 1190 as a traditional Norman style church, it has been extensively and attractively remodelled and in the mid-19th century benefited from having the architect Sir George Gilbert Scott (St Pancras Station, Albert Memorial) as a member of the congregation.

It is one of only three churches in the country to have a saddleback tower roof set transverse to the chancel and nave. Much of the stained glass is modern, although this is balanced by ancient wall paintings and a Jacobean pulpit.

From the church porch take the path that goes ½ left heading towards the right of a terrace of cottages. Go though a gap in the wall and either turn left to The Cock (PH1) or follow the footpath marked 'Chorleywood 1½' on your right through a kissing gate next to The Barn. The Cock has improved a great deal since I first regretted visiting it in the 1990s and it is now well worth a refreshing break.

From the kissing gate next to The Barn you will quickly reach a lane and metal fence. Cross to the kissing gate opposite and follow the laurel hedge downhill. The hedge becomes a metal fence and the M25 can be glimpsed in the distance. When you go through a kissing gate onto a track, quickly turn left. Passing a tennis court, you will reach and cross New Road.

The path continues along a hedge and bears right through trees. You will now go over wooden slats and then over a bridge to a bench where you turn right along an attractive stretch of the Chess. On your left you will see a water works. You will reach and cross New Road again at Bridge Cottage. Go through a kissing gate and keep to the hedge on your left.

After a kissing gate the path narrows, look out for a huge weeping willow on your right. Once beyond it, you will reach a crossing track (FP15). Here go left to a gate and immediately right to another. Now climb ½ left over a field. When you reach the field boundary hedge go left and then right through the hedge at the top of the field.

Follow the edge of Turveylane Wood to a kissing gate next to a metal 5bar gate. Now follow the track in front of you that goes to the left of a hedge until you reach another metal 5bar gate. Ignoring a footpath on your right, you have to go slightly left to follow the path around Mountgate Farm to reach a long tarmac drive.

Follow the drive until turning left on a footpath just after the entrance gates, this leads directly to The Red Lion (PH2). Nearby is a Baptist chapel dating from 1778.

Turn right from the pub and follow the road back to Chenies.

Cross the village green and go up the gravel drive to the church of St Michael.

The church houses the Bedford family chapel, the most complete set of family monuments you are likely to see.

It is adjacent to Chenies Manor that Pevsnor described as 'archaeologically a fascinating puzzle' and boasting magnificent chimneys that Henry VIII once admired. The manor and gardens are open every Wednesday and Thursday and Bank Holiday Mondays during the summer.

From the church continue along the gravel drive towards the Manor, turn right by the main gates and go between two tall brick walls.

After entering a wood, turn left on a wide track (ignoring paths straight on and ½ left). Follow the track until you reach a wooden kissing gate. Go through the gate and immediately right through a metal kissing gate. With Latimer in view, bear left along the top of the field to another kissing gate and a double line of wood / wire fences.

Continue between the fences towards Coney Wood. The path follows the edge of the wood and narrows downhill past brambles, elder bushes and nettles to a kissing gate. Go ½ left downhill over the next field and you will now see Latimer House high in front of you. Built in 1863 after the Elizabethan original burnt to the ground, it was used to interrogate prisoners during the war including Rudolph Hess.

You will reach a kissing gate near to the junction of roads to Chenies, Chesham, Little Chalfont and Latimer. Cross the road and follow the road back to Latimer.

Starting Point: The village green at Latimer

TQ003988
Explorer Map 172
Chiltern Hills East

Length:

6 miles / 9.66 kilometres

Terrain:

This is an attractive walk along the River Chess and its valley, mainly through meadows and open farmland.

Marsworth

Grand Union Canal, Reservoirs, Wendover Arm Restoration, Nature Reserve

Startop's End Reservoir

Cooks Wharf is located just over a mile north of Marsworth on the Grand Union Canal. Originally called the Grand Junction, the canal was built between 1793 – 1805 to join up separate canals to form one waterway from London to Birmingham.

The long walk starts from the car park at Cooks Wharf where you go right along the towpath passing the Dunstable & District Boat Club. To shorten the walk, start from the Red Lion in Marsworth (PH1) and join the towpath at bridge 130.

When you reach bridge 131 go up to the road and cross over to a towpath on the other side. Continue until bridge 132 and cross back to the original side. At this point an ice cream from 'Bluebells' might be good idea.

82

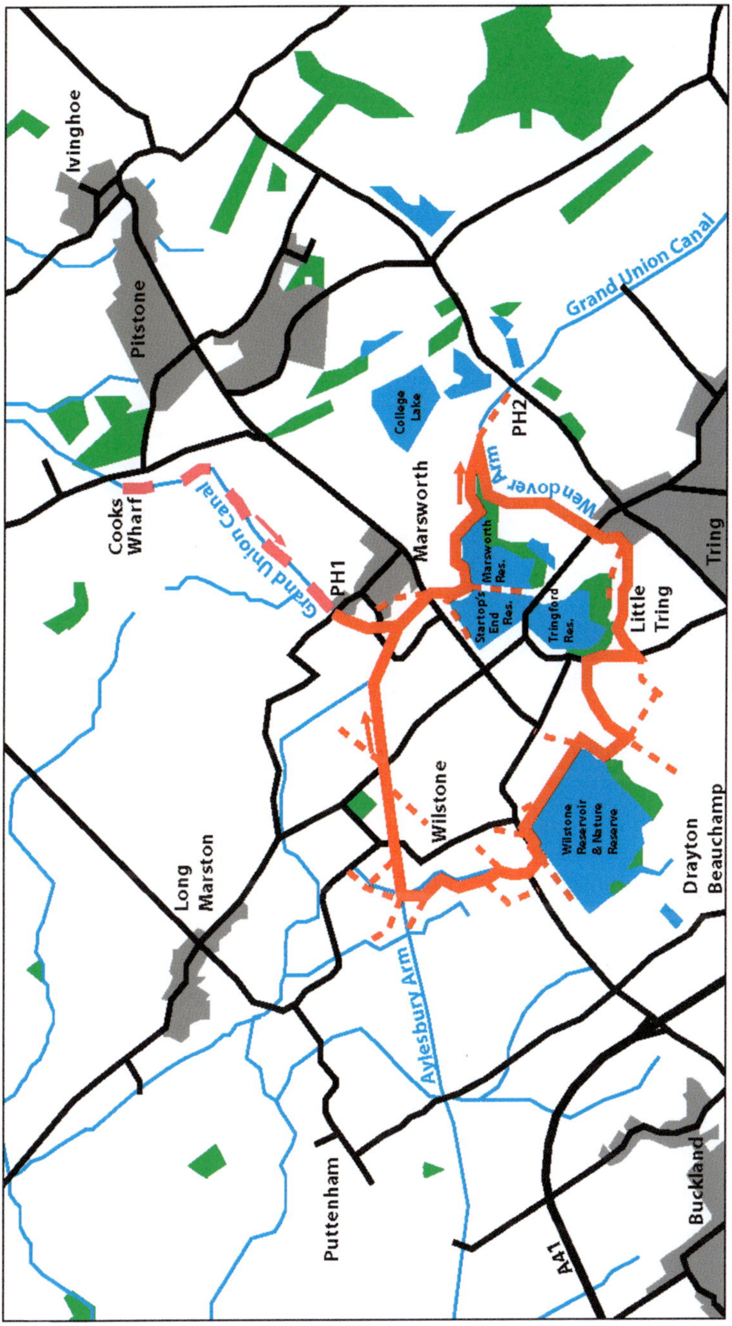
Ivinghoe
Pitstone
Cooks Wharf
Grand Union Canal
PH1
Marsworth
College Lake
PH2
Wendover Arm
Grand Union Canal
Marsworth Res.
Startop's End Res.
Tringford Res.
Little Tring
Tring
Wilstone
Wilstone Reservoir & Nature Reserve
Drayton Beauchamp
Long Marston
Aylesbury Arm
Puttenham
A41
Buckland

Continue along the canal all the way to Marsworth Top Lock 45, passing Startop's End Reservoir and Marsworth Reservoir on your right. As Tring Summit is the highest point on the canal north of London and south of Braunston in Northamptonshire, the reservoirs' function is to replenish the canal with the millions of gallons of water it requires daily.

Now turn right onto the Wendover Arm (however you can choose to continue the short distance to the Grand Junction Arms (PH2) with its canalside garden and then retrace your steps).

Construction of the Wendover Arm started in 1793, with the aim of transporting water from Wendover Springs. It was not a success due to water loss.

Wilstone Reservoir was constructed to combat the leakage but by 1897 the loss was so large that the arm was taking water from the Grand Union rather than vice versa. In 1904 it closed and is now navigable only to Little Tring. Initially a little overgrown the canal opens out into attractive countryside particularly following bridge 2. If you like digestive biscuits, take note of Heygates Mill, this is where most of the flour comes from to make them.

Go up to the road and turn right when you reach bridge 3. (Carry on under the bridge, and return to it, if you want to see the end of the navigable canal). Proceed along Little Tring Road, past the pumping station entrance and take the first footpath on the left, bearing right along the empty canal that is under restoration. Just before bridge 4 turn right through a metal kissing gate and then turn right again when you get to a track with a 5bar gate on your left. When you pass a Wilstone Reservoir Nature Reserve sign turn left and continue along the embankment before descending to a car park.

Go to the far end of the car park and onto the road, turning left and continuing the short distance to a sharp left bend.

Here cross the metal barrier on the right side of the road, go through a gate and along the hedge until going ½ right over a field to another gate.

Now go left along a track and through a metal gate. Go right, following the Black Poplar Trail sign, along the right hand edge of the field where's there a stream, until a further metal gate. You will get to a half hidden water pumping station next to a 5bar gate. Just before this building turn left along the hedge still following the Black Poplar Trail and the stream.

When the footpath forks, bear ½ right still following and eventually crossing the stream near two small sluice gates. Continue to the Aylesbury Arm of the Grand Union, where you turn right onto the towpath.

At Wilstone Bridge (the first one you pass) there is the opportunity to visit the village of Wilstone and its pub, the Half Moon. Back on the canal, continue to bridge 1 and go up to a lane and then left following the circular walk sign. It is only a short way to reach the Grand Union again (at bridge 131) where you take the towpath on your left.

To ease the journey back to Cooks Wharf, at bridge 130 go up to the lane and right to The Red Lion (PH1). Then retrace your steps, rejoin the canal and continue to the starting point.

Starting Point: Cooks Wharf

SP927161
Explorer Map 181
Chiltern Hills North

Length:

Long Walk: 8 miles / 12.88 kilometres
Short Walk: 5½ miles / 8.85 kilometres

Terrain:

Predictably flat but towpaths can be a muddy after rain.

85

Rotherfield Greys

Greys Court

Greys Court

The National Trust describes Greys Court as picturesque and intriguing. Originally 14th century, the surviving tower dates from 1347. There is a walled garden and an attractive courtyard outside, and inside some outstanding plasterwork.

If arriving by car, park on Rocky Lane, first right after passing the house coming from Henley. Walk up to the house and then, after passing the entry kiosk, go through the small car park. Follow the metal fence downhill on 'Estate Walk 2'. This is the Chiltern Way. Once through 'Johnnie's Gate' and then a kissing gate, you follow the edge of a bluebell wood. After a small wooden bridge the Chiltern Way goes left but you continue straight on.

Follow the path through two gates, passing farm buildings, to a lane. Ignore the National Trust path opposite, turn right and then after a few yards left onto another path.

Cross another lane, the path is marked 'Lower Assendon 1', and follow the white arrows.

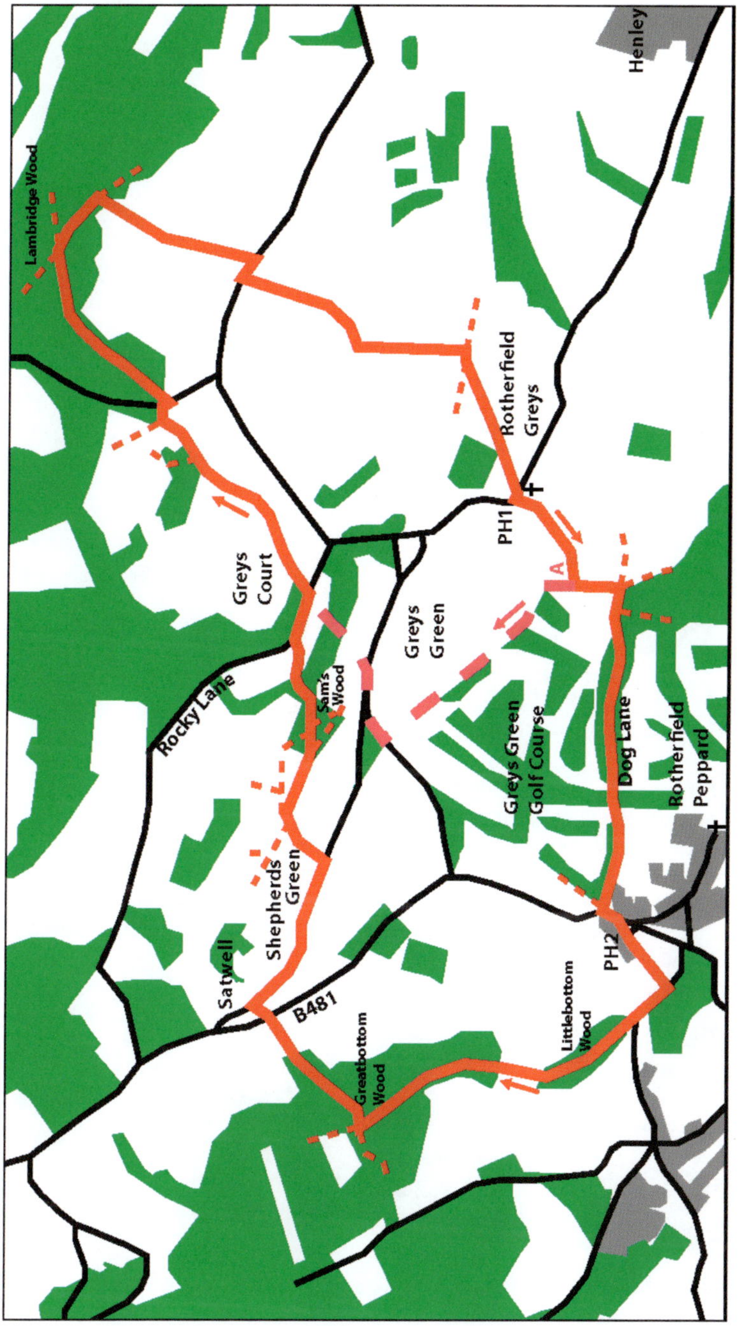
Lambridge Wood
Henley
Rotherfield
Greys
PH1
A
Greys
Court
Greys
Green
Rocky Lane
Sam's
Wood
Greys Green
Golf Course
Dog Lane
Rotherfield
Peppard
Shepherds
Green
Satwell
B481
Greatbottom
Wood
Littlebottom
Wood
PH2

This is the beautiful, if a little muddy, Lambridge Wood. After you've gone about ½ mile / .85 km, turn right onto a crossing path.

Now be cautious, you'll pass one post advising path realignment, then after 250 yds / 225 mtrs there's a wooden direction post indicating a path going left. Just before this second post, look out for a yellow arrow on a tree to your right and follow it downhill. Bear left at the bottom of the hill, going over a sunken track. Look out for the first boundary on the adjoining field to your right and then cross a stile out of the wood into the field, following the boundary through a line of oak trees

Cross a farm track and then keep straight until you meet a road. Turn right and after a short distance go left along the drive to Lime Tree Farm. When the concrete drive goes left, continue straight on.

Follow the rusty footpath signs as the track dips down along the wooded edge of a field.

At the bottom of the field turn right and then quickly left over a stile. The wire fence on your left will bend and go uphill, follow it on the well trodden but unmarked path. After 500 yds / 450 mtrs you will reach St. Nicholas Church and The Maltsters Arms (PH1) at Rotherfield Greys. The church contains the de Grey Brass commemorating Robert de Grey, the last of his line to live at Greys Court, and the very elaborate Knollys Tomb.

Walk towards The Maltsters Arms and, if you're not going for a pint, turn left down the side of the church at William's Cottage.

88

Follow the path as it passes a large woodland plantation and at the next field boundary go through a metal gate. Continue ¼ right over the field to another metal gate and a T junction with a bridleway. This is Point A.

Short Walk from Point A

Turn right on the bridleway (Chiltern Way extension) and continue for ¾ mile / 1.2 kms until reaching a busy road. Turn right along the road and after 250 yds / 225 mtrs cross a cricket field on your left to a path just to the right of the pavilion. The path is then clearly signposted as it forks right and dips into woodland, over a field, through gates installed by the Chiltern Society, and back to Rocky Lane.

On the long walk, turn left on the bridleway and, after a metal 5bar gate with a wooden gate next to it, turn right onto Dog Lane. This can be fairly muddy and, at the end of the track, turn left in front of an Italian restaurant. In front of you to the right across the road you'll see the sign for The Red Lion (PH2).

Follow the quiet road past the pub and bear right at the next crossroads. When the lane bends left, keep straight on into Littlebottom Wood.

The bridleway climbs through pleasant woodland before crossing a track into the open and then into Greatbottom Wood. Follow the tree arrows though the wood that is carpeted with bluebells in the spring.

When you reach a clearly marked crossing bridleway (there's a large tyre embedded in the earth as a kind of traffic island) turn right and climb fairly steeply to the B481. Cross straight over and take the quiet lane to The Lamb.

Formerly owned by Antony Worrall Thompson, at the time of writing The Lamb is closed but not abandoned.

Turn right and continue along the road for about 750 yds / 685 mtrs until you see a traditional telephone box. Here turn left through an attractive collection of houses. Bear right and then fork right through a metal gate adjacent to the last house. Go through one kissing gate and follow the edge of the field to another.

When you enter Sam's Wood fork left. Ignore a crossing path and then bear left, following a wooden fence to a stile. The clearer path will now bend right but you go left downhill bearing right to reach a stile. Continue along the edge of the field to reach Rocky Lane and turn right in the direction of Greys Court.

Starting Point: Rocky Lane

SU724832
Explorer Map 171
Chiltern Hills West

Length:

Long Walk: 7 miles / 11.27 kilometres
Short Walk: 4¼ miles / 6.84 kilometres

Terrain:

Only one steep hill but the bridleways can be muddy. Lovely in spring when the woodland is carpeted in bluebells.

Stoke Row

Maharajah's Gift, Philanthropist's House

Maharajah's Well

Stoke Row stands out from many of its Oxfordshire neighbours for the simple reason that it's not particularly pretty. The pub and church tick the right boxes but the village's one unique attraction is a gift from the East.

The Maharajah's Well was given to the villagers by the Maharajah of Benares, a friend of a local resident who lived and worked in India and who had sunk a well in Azimurgh to help the local community.

The maharajah returned the favour in 1863, donating the money for the construction of the 368ft deep well that served the population of Stoke Row until the Second World War. Adjacent to the well is a cherry orchard that replicates the mango grove next to the well in India.

From the entrance to the well take the footpath between Well Cottage and the cherry orchard. At the end of the path turn left onto what is Cox's Lane.

92

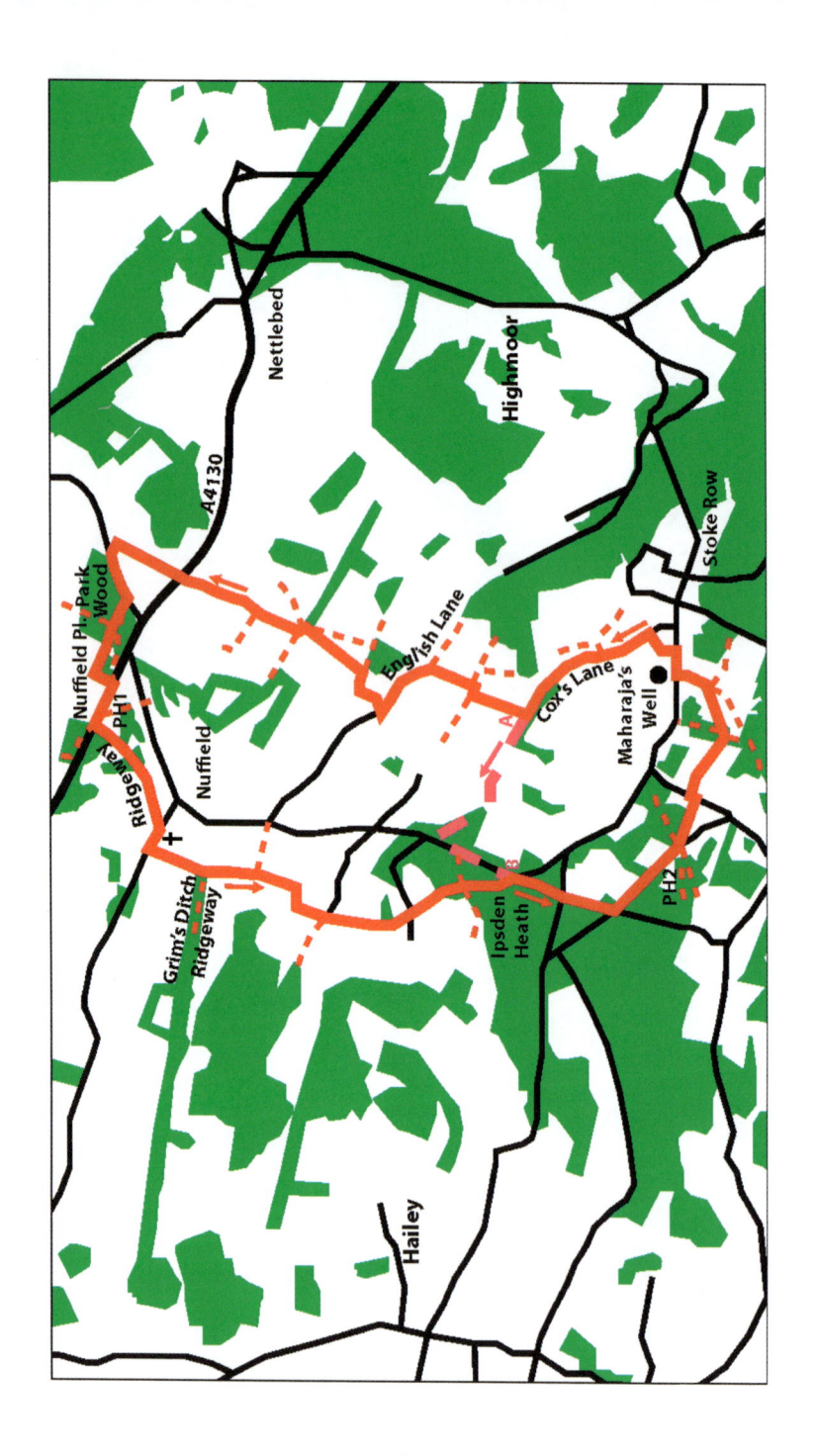

When the tarmac ends just after Plum Tree House, follow the restricted byway ¼ right. After about 730 yds / 670 mtrs look out for a stile on your right. This is Point A.

Short Walk from Point A

For the short walk, do not turn right at Point A. Follow Cox's Lane, a pleasant journey until you reach a junk yard at Kit Lane. Pass the skips and turn left on the lane at the end of the track. Now walk 650 yds / 600 mtrs to Point B.

For the long walk, turn right over the stile (if you get to a crossing farm track, you have missed the stile and gone too far) and then uphill to another, then follow a barbed wire fence. At the far end go over a stile and right. After a short distance turn left over a stile and onto a footpath that follows another wire fence. At the bottom of the field turn left (onto English Lane).

Just before you reach English Farm, you see a large barn on your right, turn towards it on a track that is only marked by a small tree arrow. Go behind the barn until forking right (unmarked) past a shed and a derelict building. You then cross a stile next to a 5bar gate and go diagonally across the field to the far corner. At the end of the field turn left onto a track and follow it quickly around to the right, walking towards a telecommunications tower and row of telegraph poles, and subsequently the A4130.

The track will change to tarmac and, on reaching the A4130, you cross over and continue straight, following the path under the telegraph poles.

At the next 5bar gate, turn left along a lane and take the first footpath on the right at Mayfield into Park Wood. Follow the main track and you emerge at Nuffield Place, the old home of Lord Nuffield who, after leaving school at 14, designed his first car in 1912 and became known as the 'English Henry Ford'.

William Morris went on to donate much of the fortune he made from the motor industry to Oxford University. He lived in Nuffield Place from 1933 – 1963 and on his death it was left to Nuffield College. The house, that is full of artefacts from his life, is now managed by the National Trust.

Turn left from the entrance, walk to the A4130 and go right the short distance to The Crown (PH1). Billing itself as the best pub in Nuffield, it is the only pub in Nuffield. Just past it you will take The Ridgeway through a collection of houses and onto Huntercombe golf course.

The path is clearly marked, initially passing the 4th tee, then over a fairway into trees. Go ½ right across another fairway and into trees again. Continue to follow the arrows, heading towards and passing the clubhouse until leaving the course through a metal kissing gate. Now go ½ left over a field towards the church.

Turn right onto a lane and just after Nuffield church turn left. You now have outstanding views of Oxfordshire. When The Ridgeway goes right following Grim's Ditch, keep straight on.

After climbing through woodland and emerging into the open, ignore a path to the left, go along the edge of the field and through a copse, and then skirt around Ridgeway Farmhouse.

The path crosses a driveway and then, at the front of the house, goes left over a field to follow a wooden fence and hedge to a lane. Cross the lane and go through the kissing gate at the far end of the field and along a wire fence.

Once through the ornate kissing gate at the end of that field, continue straight across the front of the house at Homer Farm, picking up the track that goes downhill past a barn to a T junction with another track. Cross to the kissing gate opposite and make your way downhill to another kissing gate into the copse in front of you. The narrow path is usually overgrown with nettles as you continue into the trees of Ipsden Heath. Ignore a crossing bridleway and continue straight. You start climbing and, after a track comes in from the left, the path widens and becomes muddy in winter.

At the top of the incline go left through a set of wooden poles near a small Woodland Trust sign and turn right on the road. (You can continue through the wood but the terrain can get increasingly very muddy). This is Point B.

Long and Short Walk from Point B

Turn right at a crossroads signed Ipsden and Well Place via a 'Quiet Lane'. Go straight over the next crossroads signed to nowhere and then left at the following crossroads. You then reach a pub not to be missed - The Black Horse (PH2).

There can be few pubs more isolated than this one. If you were in the desert it might be an apparition. But here it is, dispensing quality local beer in a public bar that still looks like a public bar and a lounge that looks more like a lounge than my own. There are hanging baskets and well kept gardens that are clearly well thought of by the local farming clientele. From the pub continue down the lane the short distance to a junction of paths on the left.

Take the one over a stile next to a wooden 5bar gate and follow the edge of the wood on your left until the trees end.

Keep straight on, aiming for a stile just to the left of the building in the distance. Turn left onto the lane and quickly right over two stiles. Continue with the edge of the field on your right, and then over a stile made from a tree trunk and into trees.

None of the following paths are marked but first of all go straight, along the path in front of you. You will then bear left and reach an old shack that looks like the remnants of two old railway goods carriages, continue and then turn right between two fences. Go over a stile in the fence on your left and then ½ right over two fields to a lane.

Now turn left, passing a sign for Woodside Farm and Beech End. Turn right at the road past a line of rather unattractive bungalows back to the Maharajah's Well.

Starting Point: Maharajah's Well

SU678840
Explorer Map 171
Chiltern Hills West

Length:

Long Walk: 7¾ miles / 12.47 kilometres
Short Walk: 3½ miles / 5.6 kilometres

Terrain:

A good mixture of woodland and meadow. Can be muddy in places during the winter but not too physically demanding.

Stokenchurch

Bluebell Woods, Bomber Memorial, Red Kites, Getty's Cricket Ground, Nature Reserve

Bomber Memorial

The best time to visit Cowleaze Wood is in the spring when there is a memorable display of bluebells. There was also a Sculpture Trail but this was dismantled when the money ran out. However, such an attractive vista disguises a tragedy in 1944 when a returning bomber crashed in the wood killing seven aircrew.

Take the wide path through trees opposite the entrance (1). You emerge into an open area before going under a line of telegraph poles. Now follow an arrow to re-enter the wood. Ignore L24 that goes right and, after passing a hollow, the path levels. Just by a kink in the path, look out for a small sign to the memorial (2) attached to a tree on the left. (If you see a 'Wormsley Estate Strictly Private' sign on the right, you've gone too far).

This granite stone remembers the aircrew of a Halifax bomber who, returning from a raid on Nuremberg, crashed into the hill while on their way to make an emergency landing at nearby RAF Benson. The reason is unknown but the 1000 aircraft that took part in the raid had suffered considerably due to the clear weather conditions.

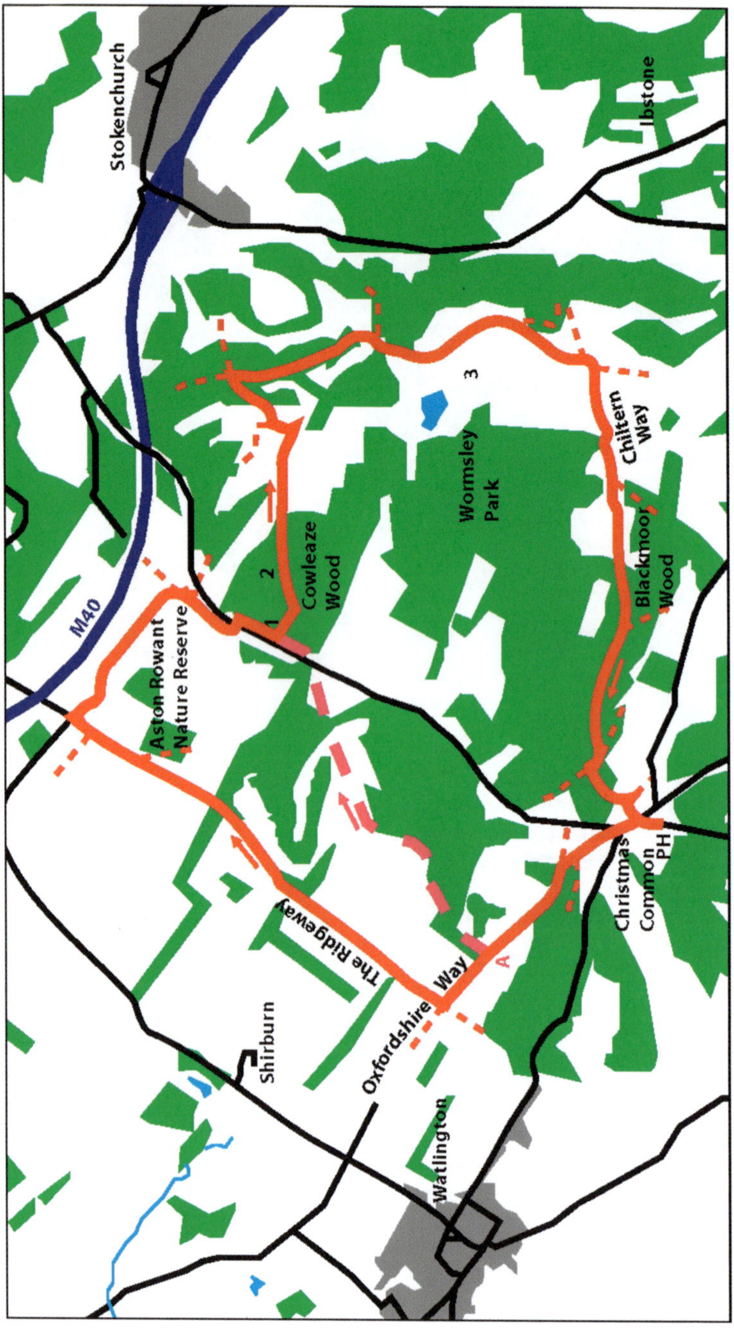
Stokenchurch
Ibstone
M40
Aston Rowant
Nature Reserve
1
2
Cowleaze
Wood
3
Wormsley
Park
Chiltern
Way
Blackmoor
Wood
Christmas
Common
PH
The Ridgeway
Oxfordshire
Way
A
Shirburn
Watlington

Retrace your steps, go left and continue until reaching a kissing gate. Now go ¼ left under telegraph wires through a gate and on to a kissing gate at the bottom of the field. You are now on the 2500 acre / 1000 ha Wormsley Estate, a bucolic heaven where Red Kites fly and deer roam, bought in 1986 by the immensely rich philanthropist and cricket lover, the late Sir Paul Getty.

Once extinct in England and Scotland, the first site where Red Kites were intended to be released was Windsor Great Park. However, in 1989 the project ran into difficulties and Getty offered Wormsley Park as an alternative. Since then they have flourished over a large portion of the Chilterns.

Turn left onto the lane (L29) and, at Lower Vicar's Farm, go right, through a gate onto L23. The path goes behind the farm to a gate where you go ½ left across a field studded with cowslips in the spring. Cross the next stile or go through a 5bar gate and continue ½ left, climbing steeply to a bridleway (L19) and turn right.

After just over ½ mile / 900 mtrs, you will reach a lane and go right. Ignore a bridleway on the left and then a signpost for 'Wormsley'. Once past the 'big' house, that is just visible on your right, the lane will bear right to a little bit of south London in the Chilterns (3).

For Getty was so enamoured with cricket, after Mick Jagger introduced him to the game, that he built his own ground based on the Oval in 1992.

You can't follow the lane up to the ground, you must bear left on the bridleway that now becomes a track. Once past the ground, keep to the wire fence on the left. Ignore a bridleway that goes straight uphill between two metal 5bar gates and enters woodland. Look out for and take another distinct narrow path just a little further on to the right of a wire fence.

You will reach a crossing path after 650 yds / 600 mtrs, next to two metal 5bar gates, that is the Chiltern Way. Here turn right and go ¼ left over the field to a kissing gate. Go over the lane to another kissing gate and ½ left to a further one next to a 5bar gate.

Turn right onto the lane and quickly left before you reach a warning sign of the 'Keep Out' variety. The Chiltern Way shortly goes left but you must keep on SH4. This clear path passes a stone urn and then winds through Blackmoor Wood. Ignore a crossing track and continue uphill to path SH6 that goes left and that you also ignore. You now have a long climb (900 yds / 823 mtrs) to meet SH5. Here bear right keeping on SH4 for a short distance before forking left onto PY3 until you reach a driveway.

Turn left past a tennis court and go in front of a house to a wire fence where you turn right. The path bears left and reaches a road. Here go ½ left towards Nettlebed and Henley, and forward to the Fox & Hounds (PH). Described by CAMRA as having a rare interior of outstanding historic interest, the pub probably hasn't changed much since the Civil War's opposing armies allegedly observed a truce on the common on Christmas Day in 1643.

When you leave the pub, turn left, returning to the crossroads in the direction of Stokenchurch and Chinnor. Continue and just past a second crossroads turn left onto the Oxfordshire Way.

Walk along the edge of the field with the hedge on your left.
After a field boundary, you ignore a path off to the left, and then bear ½ right into trees. Go through a kissing gate and then left, continuing on the Oxfordshire Way (PY4). You will reach a tarmac drive passing the Pyrton Cat Hotel and then a sawmill. This is Point A.

Shorter Walk from Point A

For the shorter walk, go right onto PY16 just past the sawmill. Don't deviate from this path until reaching and going through a wooden gate next to a metal 5bar gate. The path bears left as SH3. You follow field edges until reaching a metal gate and then go ½ right up a daunting hill. Eventually reaching a kissing gate, continue up to a track, over a stile and ¼ right over a field to the lane back to Cowleaze Wood.

To complete the longer walk keep on the drive and turn right onto The Ridgeway that crosses after a further 475 yds / 435 mtrs. Walk along the track for just over 1¾ mls / 2.82 kms going beneath a row of telegraph wires. Ignore one path going right, keep on until reaching a lane just before the M40.

Here turn right and just after Hill Farm bear left through a kissing gate onto path L14.

This is Aston Rowant National Nature Reserve that covers 400 acres / 162 ha and is composed of flower rich chalk grassland, woodland and juniper scrub. Follow the path uphill along the field edge, through another kissing gate. There are small plaques along the way explaining the scarce flora and fauna, and benches allow you to enjoy marvellous views.

After reaching a 5bar gate, go sharp right along an unused lane passing to the right of picnic benches and by an information sign emploring you to listen out to the local birdsong. At the end of the lane, cross over the road back to the Cowleaze Wood car park.

Starting Point: Cowleaze Wood Car Park Entrance

SU725956
Explorer Map 171
Chiltern Hills West

Length:

Long Walk: 9 miles / 14.42 kilometres
Shorter Walk: 7¼ miles / 11.73 kilometres

Terrain:

A full of interest walk along clear well marked paths but with several long steep inclines.

Turville

TV & Film Locations inc. Vicar of Dibley Church, Chitty Chitty Bang Bang Windmill

St Barnabus, Dibley

Turville is perhaps the most perfectly located and least spoilt Chilterns village. The producers of various TV programmes and films seem to think so, as the village has been the backdrop to various productions such as 'Went The Day Well', 'Goodnight Mr. Tom' and, perhaps most famously, 'The Vicar of Dibley'. High above the village is the windmill from the film 'Chitty Chitty Bang Bang'.

Dawn French's church, St Barnabus, is really St Mary's that has connexions with Percy Bysshe Shelley's family, the de L'Isles and the Dudleys and contains a striking window by John Piper.

Starting from the church, turn left on the road going away from The Bull & Butcher. Take the first footpath on the right opposite The Old Vicarage. Go through a kissing gate and ½ left over the field (footpath I5). At the far side go through two gates and ½ left to another.

103

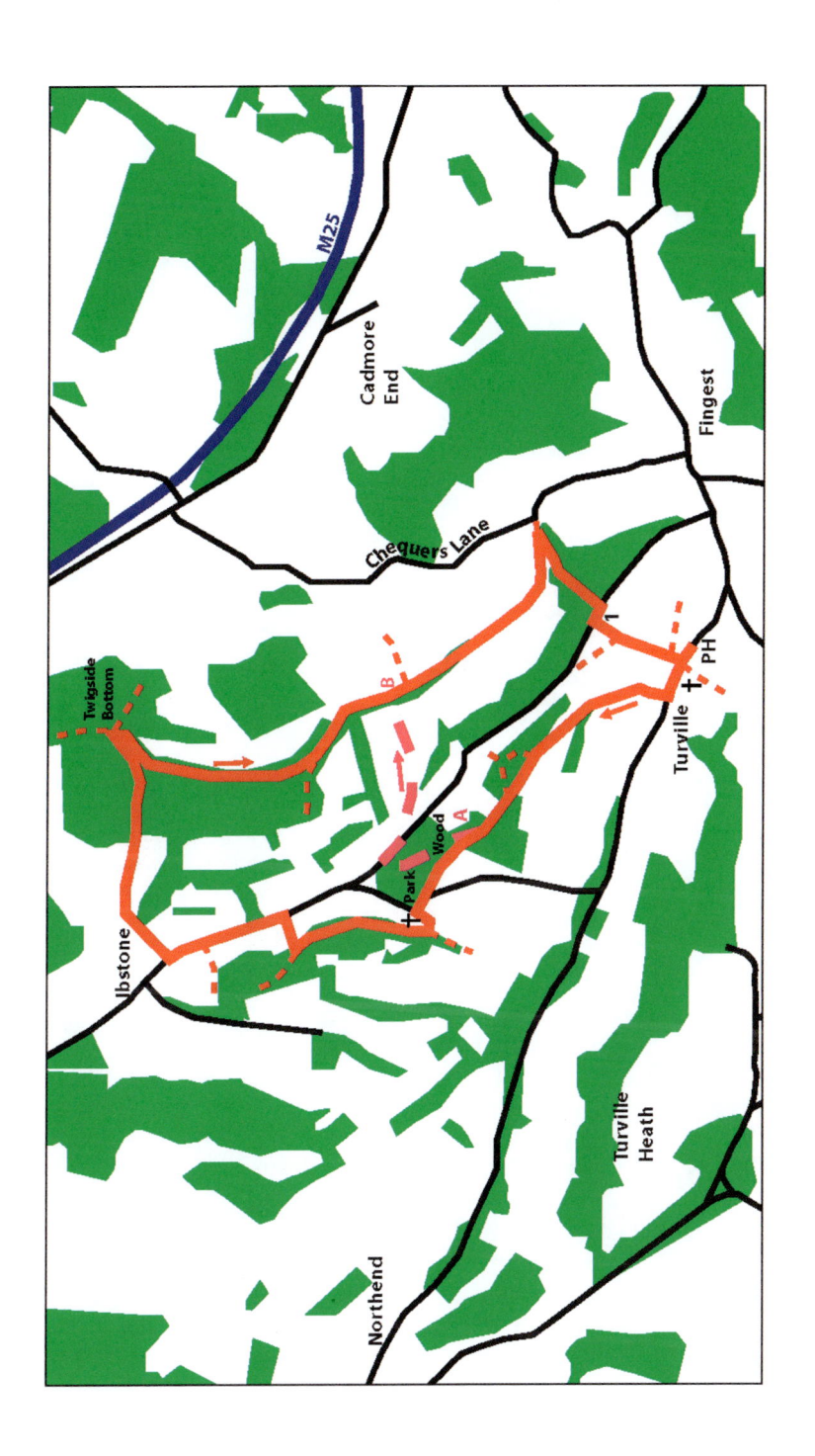

Follow the clear narrow path as it meanders through trees uphill to a kissing gate donated by the South Bucks HF Walking Club.

Then go ½ right to the top of the field to another kissing gate where you turn left following the wire fence. After a short distance ignore path I8, continue along the fence and eventually the path goes into Park Wood. Here turn left, continuing to follow I5 where I7 goes right. You reach Point A when I5 forks right. Be wary as this is easy to miss and the more distinct path that continues straight becomes I6.

Short Walk from Point A

After forking right on I5 you go through a plantation and reach more mature woodland. The path can now become difficult to follow especially in the autumn. You must look out for a stake and an arrowed tree, turn sharp right uphill and quickly deviate left to another stake. Bearing right uphill, go on to a further post and the path becomes easier to follow through the undergrowth. If you miss any of this, just head uphill towards the intermittent sound of traffic on the road to Ibstone.

This part of the walk is attractive in the spring with the woodland carpeted with bluebells. In the autumn there are plenty of blackberries. When you reach the road turn right in front of Ibstone House. At the end of a long brick wall and wooden panelled fence turn left onto a bridleway where you can collect conkers in season. Descend to a 5bar gate and then between two wooden fences, then turn right on I14 at a metal gate. This is Point B.

On the long walk, keep straight on I6 following the edge of the wood. You will eventually reach a kink in the road from Turville. Turn right onto the road and then left to St Nicholas, Ibstone. The church was once joined to the village but has been isolated probably since the Black Death.

It is located in as peaceful a setting as you can imagine and the churchyard, with clumps of daffodils, is particularly pretty on a sunny spring day. Climb the steps and follow the path past the church, and then head straight through the gravestones to the trees on the far side.

Turn right on well arrowed path (I4). When the path reaches a junction (with I3) continue on I4. Eventually turn right onto I2 and continue between two wooden fences towards a group of houses. When you reach the road, turn left, passing in front of Sonningfield. Continue on this road for just under 600 yds / 550 mtrs until you reach Ravenscroft. Here turn right, opposite Glebe Cottages and continue through a plantation to a marvellous valley view and picnic spot next to John Howard-Jones who went 'to ground' in 2005.

Continue downhill (I12), cross a track and follow arrows into a wood and the Harecramp Estate Conservation Area. At the valley bottom (Twigside Bottom) turn left as signposted and then when I12 bears left and becomes I14a, you turn practically back on yourself (not uphill on S41). This is a well worn track and you may notice a short cut to it.

Go over two crossing tracks, the second leading to a barn on your left and ignore two bridleways that come in from the right. Point B is where the second bridleway joins.

Long and Short Walk from Point B

After passing a footpath on the left, leave the main track and take the parallel path through trees on the left to avoid the worst of the mud. You soon emerge into an attractive valley. Enter trees again and just before reaching Chequers Lane you almost go back on yourself over a stile next to a 5bar gate.

From here cross the field (on path I10) to a marked post into the woods. This path becomes quite steep, joining another through a broken fence and continuing uphill to Cobstone Mill of Chitty Chitty Bang Bang fame (1). Turn right onto the road and then left through a kissing gate. There is now a great view of Turville below and you don't have to be too fortunate to observe Red Kites flying above.

Continue down to the bottom of the very steep hill and turn left to The Bull and Butcher (PH). This establishment has been rated in the Top Fifty British pubs by The Independent and has won many awards for beer and food over the years.

Built in 1550 and Grade 2 listed, it was granted a licence in 1617 when the workers from the church threatened to down tools. The name derives from the Butcher - Henry VIII and the Bullen - Anne Boleyn.

Starting Point: St Mary's Church, Turville

SU767911
Explorer Map 171
Chiltern Hills West

Length:

Long Walk: 5 miles / 8 kilometres
Short Walk: 3 miles / 4.8 kilometres

Terrain:

A walk with lots of lovely woodland. After climbing steadily to Ibstone you descend to a wooded valley and then there's a testing climb up to Cobstone Mill and down the other side, which is even steeper.

West Wycombe

Hell-Fire Caves, Church and Mausoleum, Disraeli Manor, National Trust Villages

Hell-Fire Caves

Although their provenance is unknown, the caves on the Dashwood Estate above West Wycombe were extended in the 1740s by Francis Dashwood. The reasons were firstly to create a noteworthy addition to his gardens to show off to his contemporaries and secondly to provide a sort of work creation scheme for the hard pressed residents of the village who used the chalk to build the main road to High Wycombe.

He then established the infamous Hell-Fire Club. Members included aristocrats and statesmen - Dashwood would become Chancellor of the Exchequer and Benjamin Franklin was a frequent visitor.

Start from St Lawrence Church. Medieval in origin and standing in the middle of a hill fort, it was rebuilt in 1763 by Dashwood who dispensed with the old and reconstructed it in the classical style of the new.

108

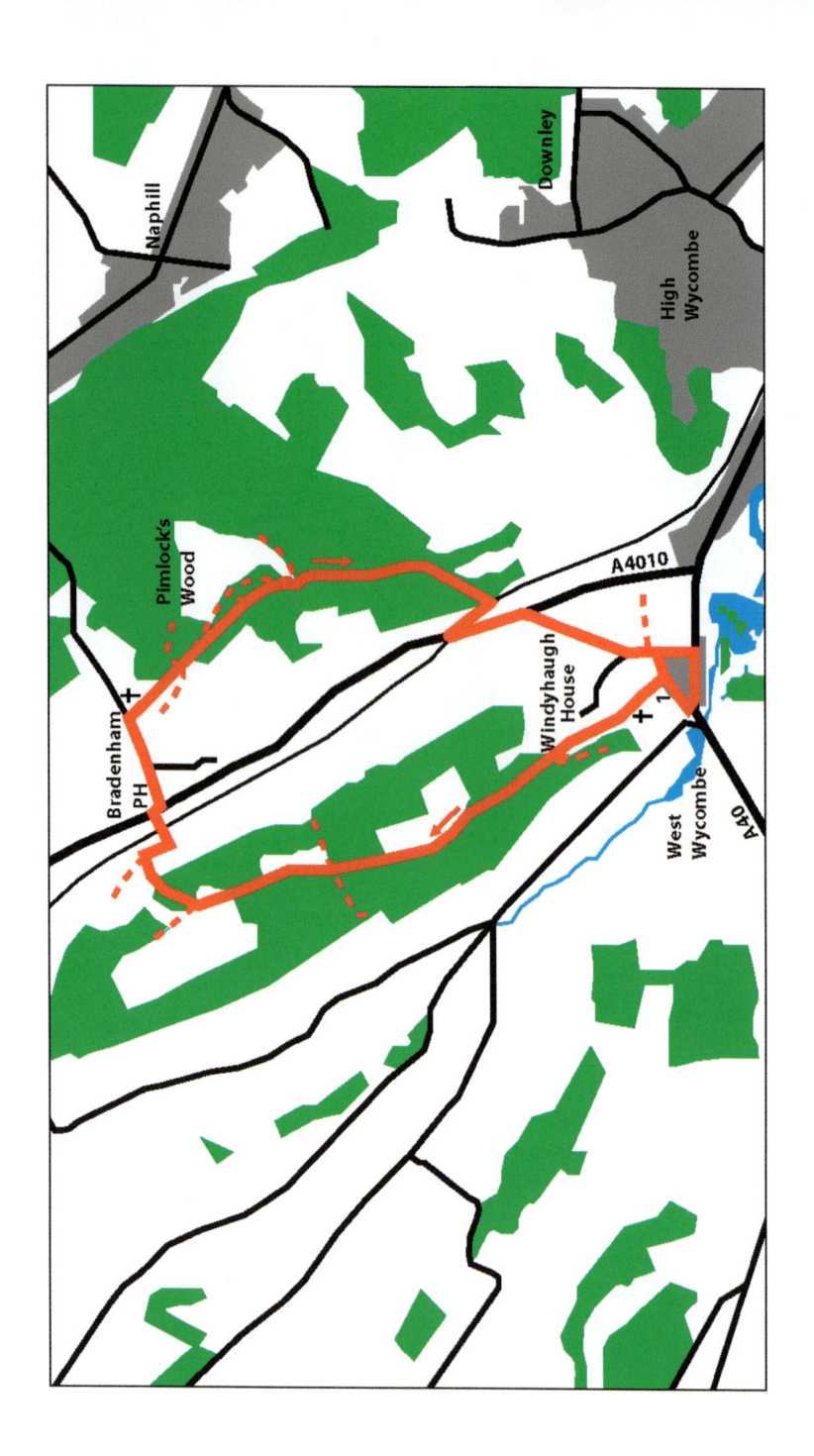

Step inside and you are greeted by a nave based on the Great Temple of the Sun in Syria with stunning plasterwork. Walk on, look up, and you will see a magnificent painting of 'The Last Supper' on the chancel ceiling.

If you can't look up there is a handily placed mirror on a trolley. In addition to the lavish decoration, there are several Dashwood memorials and perhaps the odd bit of paganism.

The most visible aspect of the building is the golden ball, in which the Hell-Fire Club are occasionally said to have held their meetings. You can have tea and climb up to the ball on summer Sundays for a stunning view of West Wycombe Park, the road to High Wycombe and the mausoleum.

Now continue to the mausoleum. Built in 1764-5 for the sum of £500 using Portland stone and flint, this was another Francis Dashwood project. After the church he had time on his hands and constructed a massive walled enclosure to display memorials to his family and friends. It is still owned by the Dashwoods.

Continue downhill to the Hell-Fire Caves. Just what kind of high jinx occurred in the tunnels, that extend for ½ mile / 0.8 km, is open to conjecture, but the caves include a banqueting hall before you reach the Inner Temple where their meetings were held.

From the caves' entrance (1) go left along the lane towards the car park and then turn right descending Church Lane to the National Trust village of West Wycombe.

As you go under the arch onto the main road note the plaque to Peter Harris who wound the church loft clock every day for 50 years. The loft is thought to have been a rest place for pilgrims and dates from the 15th century, look out for the crucifix matrix and kneeling stone on the high street side.

Saved from demolition, the village was bought by the National Trust in 1934, and is packed with notable buildings.

Pevsner describes it as a place in 'which nothing is visibly wrong', but at that time it didn't suffer from hideous amounts of traffic. Turn right from the loft and, at the road junction at the end of the village, climb to the car park next to the church either along the lane and then taking the path just beyond the caves or by the steep path up the hillside.

Go to the far end of the car park towards Windyhaugh House and take the track that leads to the left of the property. Entering working woodland that produces raw material for fences, firewood and fine furniture, you don't deviate from this well arrowed and fairly level track until it reaches a kissing gate nearly a mile from the church.

Go through the gate and onto a grassy path until you get to Nobles Farm. Turn right from the farm entrance onto a narrow path that can be easily missed and walk along a wooden fence downhill through trees. You pass a wooden gate and keep roughly straight on following a clear path to the left of a hedge. Bearing right into a clump of trees, you go through another gate and turn right following a hedge to further gate, then follow the sign to the left under the railway and onto the road.

Cross the road to The Red Lion (PH), if you fancy a pint you may be unlucky as it has quite restricted opening hours.

Continue up Bradenham Woods Lane to Bradenham village, acquired by the National Trust in 1956, its church and manor.

The church was extensively restored in 1863 and inside contains a tablet to Isaac D'Israeli (Benjamin's father) and his wife who rented the manor next door. Although dating back many centuries (Elizabeth I visited in 1566) the manor you see now is 17th century and not open to the general public.

110

From the manor's entrance continue along the brick wall and take the bridleway that goes uphill to the right of the gardens. When the brick wall goes sharply left, and the track splits in two, you take the narrow footpath leading into Pimlock's Wood to the right.

Just past a hollow there's an indistinct public footpath uphill to the left. Ignore it and keep straight on the clearer path – although the paths will meet again later on. Follow the clear path as it meanders through the wood.

Continue climbing until reaching a track. Turn left and immediately right. When you reach the meeting of two other paths, turn right. Continue on this path until just before a 'Private' sign and fork right. You now start to descend through trees to the railway track.

Previously there was a pedestrian crossing to the clear path on the other side of the valley. However you now go right following a wooden fence to Bradenham Road. Turn left under the railway bridge and continue along the road to the path that goes uphill towards the church and mausoleum.

At the top of the field follow the hedge left to a kissing gate. Here go right along the lane and quickly left up the path back to the mausoleum, church and car park.

111

Starting Point: St Lawrence Church

SU827950
Explorer Map 172
Chiltern Hills East

Length:

4 miles / 6.4 kilometres

Terrain:

The route back to the church and mausoleum car park is quite steep (climbing over 200ft) and, because of this, you may choose not to visit West Wycombe village.

Whipsnade

Tree Cathedral, War Memorial, Bronze Age Burial Site, Nature Reserve

'The Nave'

The Tree Cathedral at Whipsnade is a highly unusual, perhaps unique war memorial, one of two on this walk. Planted in 1931, based on Liverpool Cathedral and containing many different types of tree, it was designed to be a place of worship and meditation - the brainchild of EK Blyth in remembrance of three friends who died in 1918.

Approaching from the car park, you take a signed path to the left of the cathedral (1) that goes up to and through a kissing gate. Keep to the left edge of the field passing animal enclosures and go through two more kissing gates (one unused). Turn right onto a bridleway marked the Icknield Way. After ignoring a footpath off to the right you will soon be rewarded with outstanding views over Dunstable Downs.

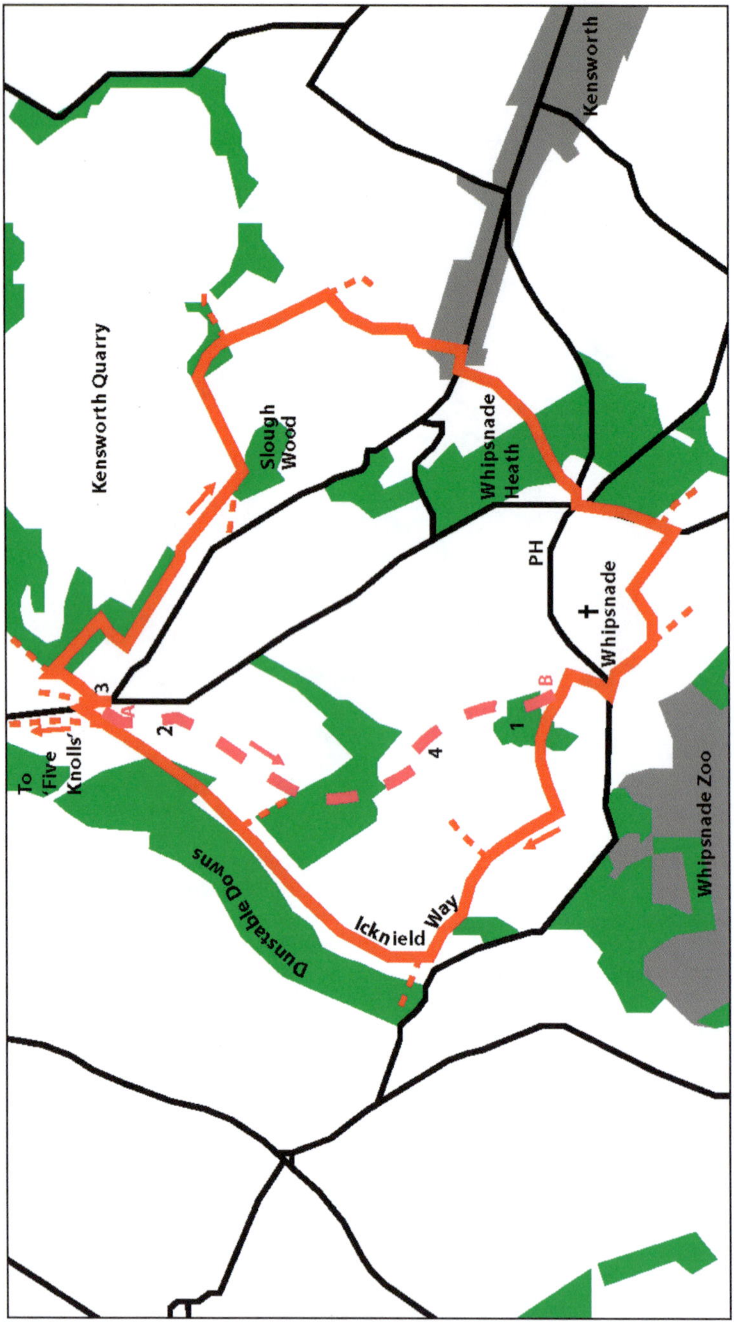
Kensworth
Kensworth Quarry
Slough Wood
Whipsnade Heath
PH
Whipsnade
Whipsnade Zoo
To 'Five Knolls'
Dunstable Downs
Icknield Way
1
2
3
4
A
B

Bear right above Bison Hill car park to a yellow topped post and go through a gate, continuing on the Icknield Way following a row of hawthorns high above the downs.

After ignoring a path off to the right leading back to the cathedral, go through a further gate. The path narrows and you will see the Chilterns Gateway Centre (2) on your right.

(Refreshment is available from the centre, there's also a gift shop from which kites are a very popular purchase in this high and windy location. What you might think is an art installation in front of the centre is in fact a 'wind catcher', part of the centre's energy saving ventilation system.)

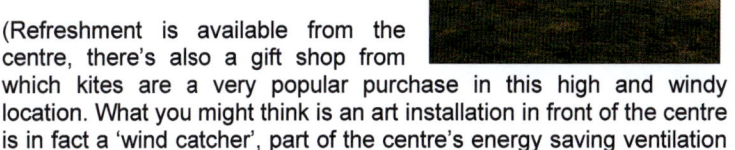

If you don't visit the centre, continue along a gravel path, passing a beacon, to a public car park near Robertson Corner.

If you have time, continue on the gravel path from the car park to 'Five Knolls', a Bronze Age burial site and the scene of a mass execution in the 5th or 6th century. There's also the remains of Norman rabbit warrens. After retracing your steps this will have added over a mile to the walk.

To reach the memorial (3) turn right on the main road to the crossroads with Isle of Wight Lane. The land around Robertson Corner was bought between 1935 and 1948 by the National Trust with money bequeathed by W. A. Robertson. The memorial is dedicated to his two brothers who were killed in the Great War. This is Point A.

Short Walk from Point A

For the easy, level short walk that takes in a small nature reserve, go to the Gateway Centre and then through the visitor car park.

Turn right onto a 'Farm Access Only' lane. Continue until a bridleway comes in from the right and a footpath goes left. Take the footpath.

Ignore a bridleway to the left when you pass an electricity sub-station. At Ever Green Lodge the surface changes to tarmac and just past an expensive housing estate you turn left into Sallowsprings Nature Reserve (4).

Follow the path through this meadow, rich in wild flowers and insects during the summer, and it will rejoin the lane. A short distance further, go right and either enter the Tree Cathedral through a kissing gate or walk through the Jubilee Orchard to the car park.

For the long walk, retrace your steps from the memorial towards the public car park. Practically opposite the car park entrance is a footpath into trees, the signpost indicates this is towards West Hill. (There is also a path going ½ left that you ignore). After passing through a metal barrier take a path that goes off to the right at a yellow post and then turn right when you reach the boundary fence of Kensworth Quarry.

When you reach the driveway to the quarry turn right and then left before you get to Isle of Wight Lane. The path will bear left and then right to follow the edge of Slough Wood with the quarry workings on your left.

The path dips downhill and follows the edge of the field to no less than three sign posts pointing you in the correct direction along the boundary of the next field.

At the end of the field you will enter trees and follow the clear path uphill to a metal kissing gate. Follow the Whipsnade Circular Walk sign through the kissing gate and then walk along the top of the field. After passing a disused kissing gate, go ½ right downhill to another one that is overgrown but next to a permanently open 5bar gate. Turn right, passing an old corrugated iron barn.

The track goes uphill through a metal 5bar gate and, just before entering a farmyard, the path goes through a gate in the hedge on your left. You will soon reach a road, turn right past Old Greenend Farm and then, after a short distance, left through a kissing gate.

116

Go straight across the field to another kissing gate and then through the trees of Whipsnade Heath on a well marked path until reaching a picnic area and car park.

Now take the road to Studham and Hemel Hempstead. Not the most pleasant part of the walk but it is only for 300 yds / 275 mtrs.

After passing a footpath on the left, you take a path on the right through a kissing gate half hidden by brambles. Follow the left edge of the field and at the end of it, before going through a metal 5bar gate, turn left through a kissing gate hidden in the hedge marked 'Chiltern Way'. (Keep straight on if you want to visit the church).

At the next kissing gate turn right along a quiet lane. On reaching Chequers House bear right past the old Post Office up to the main road. Cross the road back to the Tree Cathedral or go right to the Old Hunters Lodge (PH).

Starting Point: Tree Cathedral car park

TL009180
Explorer Map 181
Chiltern Hills North

Length:

Long Walk: 4¾ miles / 7.59 kilometres
Short Walk: 3 miles / 4.84 kilometres

Terrain:

No really challenging inclines and great views.

Printed in Great Britain
by Amazon.co.uk, Ltd.,
Marston Gate.